The History of Timon of Athens, the Man-hater Altered by Mr. Shadwell

THE

HISTORY

OF

TIMON *of* ATHENS,

THE

MAN-HATER

Altered by Mr. SHADWELL.

LONDON:
Printed for the Bookfellers in Town, and Country.

———

MDCCXL.

To the moſt Illuſtrious PRINCE

GEORGE,

Duke of *Buckingham.*

May it pleaſe your Grace,

Othing could ever contribute more to my having a good Opinion of myſelf, than the being favour'd by your Grace: The Thought of which has ſo exalted me, that I can no longer conceal my Pride from the World; but muſt publiſh the Joy I receive in having ſo noble a Patron, and one ſo excelling in Wit and Judgment; Qualities which even your Enemies could never doubt of, or detract from, and which make all good Men and Men of Senſe admire you, and none but Fools

and

and ill Men fear you for 'em. I am extreamly ſenſible what Honour it is to me, that my Writings are approved by your Grace, who, in your own, have ſo clearly ſhewn the Excellency of Wit and Judgment in your ſelf, and ſo juſtly the Defect of 'em in others, that they at once ſerve for the greateſt Example and the ſharpeſt Reproof. And no Man who has perfectly underſtood the *Rehearſal*, and ſome other of your Writings, if he has any *Genius* at all, can write ill after it.

I pretend not of an Epiſtle to make a Declamation upon theſe and your other excellent Qualities ; for naming the Duke of *Buckingham* is enough , who cannot have greater Commendations from me, than all who have the Honour to know him already give him. Amongſt which Number I think it my greateſt Happineſs to be one ; and can never be prouder of any Thing can arrive to me, than of the Honour of having been admitted ſometimes into your Grace's Converſation, the moſt charming in the World. I am now to preſent your Grace with this Hiſtory of *Timon*, which you were pleaſed to

                                tell

tell me you liked; and it is the more worthy of you, ſince it has the inimitable Hand of *Shakeſpear* in it, which never made more maſterly Strokes than in this. Yet I can truly ſay, I have made it into a Play, which I humbly lay at your Feet, begging the Countenance of your Favour, which no Man can value more than I ſhall ever do, who am unfeignedly,

    My Lord,

       Your Grace's

          Moſt Obedient

            Humble Servant,

              Tho. Shadwell.

PROLOGUE.

SInce the bare Gleanings of the Stage are grown
    The only Portion for brisk Wits o'th' Town,
We mean such as have no Crop of their own;
Methinks you should encourage them that sow,
Who are to watch and gather what does grow.
Thus a poor Poet must maintain a Muse,
As you do Mistresses for others Use
The wittiest Play can serve him but one Day,
Tho' for three Months it finds you what to say.
Yet you your Creditors of Wit will fail,
And never pay, but borrow on and rail
Poor Eccho's can repeat Wit, tho' they've none,
Like Bag-pipes they no Sound have of their own,
Till some into their Emptiness be blown.
Yet————
To be thought Wits and Judges they're so glad,
And labour for't, as if they were Wit mad
Some will keep Tables for the Wits o'th' Nation,
And Poets eat them into Reputation.
Some Scriblers will Wit their whole Bus'ness make,
For labour'd Dulness grievous Pains will take,
And when with many Throes they've travail'd long,
They now and then bring forth a foolish Song.
One Fop all modern Poets will contemn,
And by this Means a parlous Judge will seem.
Wit is a common Idol, and in vain
Fops try a thousand ways the Name to gain.
Pray judge the nauseous Farces of the Age,
And meddle not with Sense upon the Stage;
To you our Poet not one Line submits,
Who such a Coil will keep to be thought Wits:

PROLOGUE.

'Tis you who truly are so he would please,
But knows it is not to be done with Ease.
In th' Art of judging you as wise are grown
As in their Choice some Ladies of the Town.
Your neat shap'd Barbary Wits you will despise,
And none but lusty Sinewy Writers prize.
Old English Shakespear Stomachs you have still,
And judge as our Fore-fathers writ with Skill.
You coin the Wit, the Witlings of the Town
Retailers are, that spread it up and down,
Set but your Stamp upon't, tho' it be Brass,
With all the Wou'd-be-Wits, 'twill current pass:
Try it To-day, and we are sure 'twill hit,
All to your Sov'reign Empire must submit.

Dramatis

Dramatis Personæ.

TIMON *of* Athens.	Mr. *Betterton.*
Alcibiades, *an* Athenian *Captain*.	Mr *Smith.*
Apemantus, *a rigid Philosopher*.	Mr. *Harris.*
Nicias,	Mr. *Standford.*
Phæax,	Mr *Underhill.*
Ælius, *Senctors of* Athens.	Mr. *Leigh.*
Cleon,	Mr. *Norris.*
Isander,	Mr. *Percival.*
Isidore,	Mr. *Gillo.*
Thrasillus,	
Demetrius, Timon's *Steward,*	Mr *Medburne.*
Diphilus, *Servant to* Timon.	Mr *Bowman.*
Old Man.	Mr *Richards.*
Poet	Mr *Jevon.*
Pavnter.	
Jeweller.	
Musician.	
Merchant	

Evandra.	Mrs. *Bettertou*
Melissa	Mrs. *Shadwell.*
Chloe	Mrs. *Gibbs.*
Thais, *Mistresses to* Alcibiades.	Mrs. *Seymour*
Phrinias,	Mrs. *Le-Grand.*

Servants, Messengers, several Masqueraders, Soldiers.

SCENE *ATHENS.*

TIMON
OF
ATHENS.

ACT I. SCENE I.

Enter Demetrius.

Demetrius

 OW ftrange it is to fee my riotous Lord
With carelefs Luxury betray himfelf!
To feaft and revel all his Hours away ;
Without account how faft his Treafure ebbs,
How flowly flows, and when I warn'd him of
His following Dangers, with his rigorous Frowns
He nipt my growing Honefty i'th' Bud,
And kill'd it quite ; and well for me he did fo.
It was a barren Stock would yield no Fruit :
But now, like evil Counfellours, I comply,
And lull him in his foft Lethargick Life,
And like fuch curfed Politicians can

X   Share

Share in the headlong Ruine, and will rife by't :
What vaft Rewards to naufeous Flatterers,
To Pimps and Women what Eftates he gives !
And fhall I have no Share ? Begone all Honefty,
Thou foolifh, flender, thread-bare, ftarving thing begone !

Enter Poet

Here's a Fellow-Horfe-leech : How now, Poet, how
goes the World ?

Poet. Why, it wears as it grows : But is Lord *Timon*
vifible ?

Dem. He'll come out fuddenly, what have you to
prefent him ?

Poet. A little Offspring of my fruitful Mufe. She's in
travel daily for his Honour.

Dem. For your own Profit, you grofs Flatterer.
By his damn'd Panegyricks he has written   [*Afide.*
Himfelf up to my Lord's Table,
Which he feldom fails , nay, into his Chariot,
Where he in publick does not blufh to own
The fordid Scribler

Poet. The laft thing I prefented my noble Lord was
Epigram · But this is in Heroick Style.

Dem. What d'ye mean by Style ; that of good Senfe is
all alike ; that is to fay, with apt and eafie Words, not
one too little or too much; And this I think good Style

Poet O Sir, you are wide o'th' Matter ! apt and eafie !
Heroicks muft be lofty and high-founding ,
No eafie Language in Heroick Verfe
'Tis moft unfit for fhould I name a Lion,
I muft not in Heroicks call him fo !

Dem. What then ?

Poet. I'd as foon call him an Afs   No thus——
The fierce *Numidian* Monarch of the Beafts.

Dem. That's lofty, is it ?

Poet. O yes ! but a Lion would found fo baldly, not to
be endur'd, and a Bull too——but
The mighty Warrior of the horned Race.
Ah !——how that founds !

Dem. Then I perceive Sound's the great Matter in this
way

Poet.

Poet. Ever while you live.

Dem. How would you found a Fox, as you call it?

Poet. A Fox is but a scurvy Beast for Heroick Verse.

Dem. Hum—is it so? how will a Raven do in Heroick?

Poet. Oh! very well, Sir

That black and dreadful Fate-denouncing Fowl.

Dem. An excellent Sound!—But let me see your Piece.

Poet. I'll read it--'tis a good morrow to the Lord *Timon.*

Dem. Do you make good morrow found loftily?

Poet. Oh! very loftily.

The fringed Vallance of your Eyes advance,
Shake off your canopy'd and downy Trance:
Phœbus already quaffs the Morning Dew.
Each does his daily Leafe of Life renew.

Now you shall hear Defcription, 'tis the very Life of Poetry.

He darts his Beams on the Lark's mosy Houfe,
And from his quiet Tenement does rouze
The little charming and harmonious Fowl,
Which fings its Lump of Body to a Soul:
Swiftly it clambers up in the fleep Air
With warbling Throat, and makes each Note a Stair.

There's Rapture for you! hah!——

Dem. Very fine!

Poet. *This the follicitous Lover strait alarms,*
Who too long flumber'd in his Cælia's Arms:
And now the fwelling Spunges of the Night
With aking Heads flagger from their Delight:
Slovenly Taylors to their Needles haste:
Already now the moving Shops are plac'd
By those who crop the Treafures of the Fields,
And all thofe Gems the rip'ning Summer yields.

Who d'ye think they are now? Why——Nothing but
Herb-Women · There are fine lofty Expreffions for Herb
Women! ha! Already now, &c.

Dem.

Dem But what's all this to my Lord ?

Poet. No that's true, 'tis Defcription though

Dem. Yes, in twenty Lines to defcribe to him that 'tis about the Fourth Hour in the Morning——I'll in and let him know in three Words 'tis the Seventh [*Exit* Demet.

Enter Mufician

Poet Good Morning, Sir whither this way ?

Muf To prefent his Honour with a Piece of Mufick.

Enter Demetrius.

Dem My Lord will foon come out.

Poet He's the very Spirit of Nobility——
And like the Sun, whenever he breaks for h,
His univerfal Bounty falls on all

Enter Merchant, Jeweller, Painter. *and feveral others.*

Jewel Good morrow, Gentlemen.

Paint Save you all.

Dem Now they begin to fwarm about the Houfe '

Poet What Confluence the worthy *Timon* draws '
' Ingick of Bounty——Thefe familiar Spirits
Are conjur'd up by thee

Jewel 'Tis a fplendid Jewel.

Jew ' 'Tis of an excellent Water.

Poet What h ve you there, Sir ?

Paint. It is a Picture, Sir, a dumb Piece of Poetry :
But you prefent a fpeaking Poem

Poet. I have a little thing flipt idly from me:
The Fire within the Flint fhews not itfelf,
Till it be ftruck ; our gentle Flame provokes
It felf———

Dem. You write fo fcurvily, the Devil's in any Man that provokes you but yourfelf.

Poet It is a pretty Mocking of the Life.

Paint. So, fo

Dem Now muft thefe Rafcals be prefented all,
As if they had fav'd his Honour, or his Life ;
And I muft have a Feeling in the Bufinefs.

Enter certain Senators *who go in to* Timon.

Poet. How this Lord is follow'd !

[*Enter more who pafs over.*

Paint. See more, well, he's a noble Spirit '

Jewel.

Jewel. A moſt worthy Lord!

Poet. What a Flood of Viſitors his Bounty draws!

Dem. You ſee all Conditions, how all Minds,
As well of glib and ſlippery Creatures, as
Of grave and auſtere Quality, preſent
Their Services to Lord *Timon*'s proſp'rous Fortune,
He to his good and gracious Nature does ſubdue
All ſorts of Tempers, from the ſmooth-fac'd Flatterer
To *Apemantus*, that Philoſophical Churl
Who hates the World, and does almoſt abhor
Himſelf——

Paint. He is a moſt excellent Lord, and makes the
fineſt Picture !

Poet. The Joy of all Mankind; he deſerves a *Homer*
for his Poet.

Jewel A moſt accompliſh'd Perſon !

Poet. The Glory of the Age!

Paint. Above all Parallel !

Dem. And yet theſe Rogues, were this Man poor, would
fly him, as I would them, if I were he.   [*Soft Muſick.*

Poet. Here's excellent Muſick !
In what Delights he melts his Hours away ?

Enter Timon *and* Senators, Timon *addreſſing himſelf*
courteouſly to all

Tim. My Lord, you wrong yourſelf, and 'bate too
much of your own Merits : 'Tis but a Trifle.

Ælius. With more than common Thanks I muſt receive it.

Iſidore. Your Lordſhip has the very Soul of Bounty.

Phæax. You load us with too many Obligations.

Tim. I never can oblige my Friends too much.
My Lord, I remember you the other Day
Commended a Bay Courſer which I rode on.
He's yours, becauſe you lik'd him.

Phæax I beſeech your Lordſhip pardon me in this.

Tim. My Word is paſt. Is there aught elſe you like ?
I know, my Lord, no Man can juſtly praiſe
But what he does affect, and I muſt weigh
My Friends Affections with my own .
So kindly I receive your Viſits, Lords,

X 3

My

My Heart is not enough to give, methinks
I could deal Kingdoms to my Friends, and ne'er be weary.
Ælius. We all muſt ſtand amaz'd at your vaſt Bounty!
Cleon. The Spirit of Magnificence reigns in you!
Phæax. Your Bounty's as diffuſive as the Sea.
Tim My noble Lords, you do me too much Honour.
Iſand. There lives not ſuch a noble Lord on Earth.
Thraſil None but the Sun and he oblige without
A Proſpect of Return.

      Enter a Meſſenger, and whiſpers Timon.
Tim Lampridius impriſon'd! ſay you?
Meſſ. Yes, my good Lord, Five Talents is his Debt,
His Means are ſhort, his Creditors moſt ſtrict,
He begs your Letter to thoſe cruel Men,
That may preſerve him from his utter Ruine.
Tim I am not of that Temper, to ſhake off
My Friend when moſt he needs me. I know him,
A Gentleman that well deſerves my Help;
Which he ſhall have: I'll pay the Debt and free him.
Meſſ. Your Lordſhip ever binds him to your Service.
Tim Commend me to him, I will ſend his Ranſom,
And when he's free, bid him depend on me :
'Tis not enough to help the Feeble up,
But to ſupport him after——tell him ſo.
Meſſ All Happineſs to your Honour.   [*Ex. Meſſenger.*
      Enter an Old Athenian.
Old Man My Lord, pray hear me ſpeak.
Tim Freely, good Father.
Old Man You have a Servant nam'd *Diphilus.*
Tim I have ſo, that is he.
Old Man. That Fellow there by Night frequents my
      Houſe ;
I am a Man that from my firſt have been
Inclin'd to Thrift, and my Eſtate deſerves
A nobler Heir than one that holds a Trencher.
Tim. Go on.
Old Man. I have an only Daughter ; no Kin elſe,
On whom I may confer what I have got :
The Maid is fair, o'th' youngeſt for a Bride,
And I have bred her at my deareſt coſt.

                                          This

This Man attempts her Love ; pray, my good Lord,
Join with me to forbid him ; I have often
Told him my Mind in vain.

Tim. The Man is honeft.

Old Man. His Honefty rewards him in himfelf ;
It muft not bear my Daughter.

Tim. Does fhe love him ?

Old Man. She is young and apt.

Tim. Do you love her?

Diph. Yes, my good Lord, and fhe accepts of mine.

Old Man. If to her Marriage my Confent be wanting,
I call the Gods to witnefs, I will make
The Beggars of the Street my Heirs, ere fhe
Shall have a Drachma.

Tim. This Gentleman of mine has ferv'd me long ;
There is a Duty from a Mafter too :
To build his Fortune, I will ftrain a little ;
Whate'er your Daughter's Portion weighs, this Man's
Shall counterpoife

Old Man. Say you fo, my Noble Lord !
Upon your Honour this, then fhe is his.

Tim. Give me thy Hand : My Honour on my Promife.

Diph. My Noble Lord, I thank you on my Knees :
May I be as miferable as I fhall be bafe
When I forget this moft furprizing Favour :
No Fortune or Eftate fhall e'er be mine,
Which I'll not humbly lay before your Feet.

Tim. Rife——I ne'er do Good with Profpect of Return,
That were but merchandizing, a mere Trade
Of putting Kindnefs out to Ufe.

Poet. Vouchfafe
T' accept my Labours, and long live your Lordfhip.

Tim. I thank you ; you fhall hear from me anon :
What have you there, my Friend ?

Paint. A Piece of Limning for your Lordfhip.

Tim. 'Tis welcome. I like it, and you fhall find I do.

Jewel. My Lord, here is the Jewel !

Tim. 'Tis excellent !

            Enter Apemantus.

Jewel. Your Lordfhip mends the Jewel by the wearing.

                              Tim.

Tim. Well mock'd.

Poet. No, my good Lord, he speaks what all Men think.

Apem. Scum of Flatterers, wilt thou still persist
For filthy Gain, to gild and varnish o'er
This great Man's Vanities!

Tim. Nay, now we must be chidden.

Poet. I can bear with your Lordship.   [*Timon,*

Apem. Yes, and without him too: Vain, credulous
If thou believ'st this Knave, thou art a Fool.

Tim. Well, gentle *Apemantus,* good-morrow to thee.

Apem. Till I am gentle, stay for thy good-morrow;
Till thou art *Timon*'s Dog, and these Knaves honest.

Tim. Why dost thou call them Knaves?

Apem. They're *Athenians,* and I'll not recant;
They're all base Fawners; what a Coile is here
With smiling, cringing, jutting out of Bums:
I wonder whether all the Legs they make
Are worth the Sums they cost you; Friendship's full
Of Dregs; base, filthy Dregs   Thus honest Fools
Lay out their Wealth for Cringes.

Ælius Do you know us, Fellow?

Apem Did I not call you by your Names?

Tim. Thou preachest against Vice, and thou thyself
art proud, *Apemantus.*

Apem Proud! that I am not *Timon.*

Tim. Why so?

Apem To give Belief to flatt'ring Knaves and Poets,
And to be still myself the greatest Flatterer:
What should great Men be proud of 'stead of Noise
And Pomp and Show, and holding up their Heads,
And cocking of their Noses; pleas'd to see
Base smiling Knaves, and cringing Fools bow to 'em?
Did they but see their own ridiculous Folly,
Their mean and absurd Vanities; they'd hide
Their Heads within some dark and little Corner,
And be afraid that every Fool should find 'em.

Tim Thou hast too much Sow'rness in thy Blood.

Poet Hang him,——ne'er mind him——

Apem. What is this foolish Animal Man, that we
Should magnifie him so? A little warm

And

And walking Earth, that will be Aſhes ſoon;
We come into the World crying and ſqualling.
And ſo much of our Time's conſum'd in driv'ling Infancy,
In Ignorance, Sleep, Diſeaſe, and Trouble, that
The Remainder is not worth the being rear'd to.

Phæax A preaching Fool'

Apem A Fool? if thou had'ſt half my Wit, thou'dſt find
Thyſelf an Aſs! Is it not Truth I ſpeak!
Are n't all the Arts and Subtleties of Men,
All their Inventions, all their Sciences,
All their Diverſions, all their Sports, little enough
To paſs away their happieſt Hours with,
And make a heavy Life be borne with Patience?

Tim. I, with the Help of Friends, will make mine eaſier
Than what your Melancholly frames.

Apem. How little do'ſt thou look before thee!
Thou, who takes
Such great Felicity in Fools and Knaves,
And in thy own Enjoyments, wilt, ere long,
Find 'em ſuch thin, ſuch poor and empty Shadows,
That thou wilt wiſh thou never had'ſt been born.

Tim. I do not think ſo.

Phæax. Hang him, ſend him to the *Areopagus*, and let
him be whipt!

Apem. Thus Innocence, Truth and Merit often ſuffer,
Whilſt Injuries, Oppreſſors, and deſertleſs Fools
Swell in their brief Authority, look big,
And ſtrut in Furs; 'tis a foul Shame,
But 'tis a loathſome Age,——it has been long
Impoſthumating with its Villainy;
And now the Swelling's broken out
In moſt contagious Ulcers, no Place free
From the deſtructive Peſtilence of Manners;
Out upon't! 'tis time the World ſhould end!

Tim Do not rail ſo——'tis to little Purpoſe.

Apem. I fear it is, I have done my Morning Lecture,
And I'll begone——

Tim. Whither?

Apem To knock out an honeſt *Athenian*'s Brains.

Tim. Why. That's a Deed thou'lt die for, *Apemantus.*

Apem.

Apem. Yes, if doing nothing be Death by the Law.

Tim. Will nothing pleafe thee? how doft thou like this
Picture?

Apem. Better than the Thing 'twas drawn for;
'Twill neither lie, drink, nor whore,
Flatter a Man to his Face, and cut
His Throat behind his Back;
For fince falfe Smiles, and bafe Difhonour
Traffique with Man's Nature,
He is but mere Out-fide; Pictures are
Even fuch as they give out: Oh! did you fee
The Infides of thefe Fellows Minds about you,
You'd loath the bafe Corruptions more than all
The putrid Excrements their Bodies hide.

Ælius Silence the foul-mouth'd Villain.

Tim. He hurts us not How lik'ft thou this Jewel?

Apem. Not fo well as Plain-dealing, which will not coft
a Man a Doit.

Tim What doft thou think this Jewel worth?

Apem. What Fools efteem it, 'tis not worth my thinking.
Lo, now the mighty Ufe of thy great Riches!
That muft fet infin te Value on a Bauble!
Will't keep thee warm, or fatisfy thy Thirft,
Or Hunger? No, it is Comparifon
That gives it Value, then thou look'ft upon
Thy Finger, and art very proud to think
A poor Man cannot have it. Childifh Pleafure!
What ftretcht Inventions muft be found to make
Great Wealth of Ufe! Oh! that I were a Lord!

Tim What would'ft thou do?

Apem I would cudgel
Two Men a Day flattering me, till I
Had beaten the whole Senate.

Phæax. Let the Villain
Be foundly punifh'd for his licentious Tongue.

Tim No, the Man is honeft, 'tis his Humour. 'Tis odd,
And methinks pleafant. You muft dine with me,
Apemantus.

Apem I devour no Lords.

Tim. No, if you did, the Ladies would be angry.

Apem,

Apem. Yet they, with all their modeft Simperings
And varnifh'd Looks, can fwallow Lords, and get
Great Bellies by't, yet keep their virtuous Vizors
On, till a poor little Baftard fteals into
The World, and tells a Tale.

Enter Nicias. [Arms!

Tim My noble Lord, welcome! moft welcome to my
You are the Fountain from which all my Happinefs
Did fpring! your matchlefs Daughter, fair *Meliffa.*

Nic. You honour us too much, my Lord   [light

Tim. I cannot, fhe is the Joy of *Athens!* the chief De-
Of Nature, the only Life I live by: Oh, that her Vows
Were once expir'd! It is methinks, an Age
Till that bleft Day when we fhall join our Hands
And Hearts together.

Nic. 'Tis but a Week, my Lord.

Tim. 'Tis a Thoufand Years.

Apem Thou miferable Lord, haft thou, to compleat
All thy Calamities, that Plague of Love,
That moft unmanly Madnefs of the Mind,
That fpecious Cheat, as falfe as Friendfhip is?
Did'ft thou but fee how like a fniveling thing
Thou look'ft and talk'ft, thou would'ft abhor to laugh at
Thy own admir'd Image.

Tim. Peace: I will hear no Railing on this Subject.

Apem. *Oh vile corrupted Time! that Men fhould be*
       Deaf to good Counfel not to Flattery!

Tim. Come, my dear Friends, let us now vifit our Gardens,
And refrefh ourfelves with fome cool Wines and Fruit:
I am tranfported with your Vifits!
There is not now a Prince whom I can envy,
Unlefs it be that he can more beftow
Upon the Men he loves.

Ælius. My Noble Lord, who would not wed your
Friendfhip, tho' without a Dowry?

Ifid Moft worthy *Timon!*
Who has a Life you may not call your own?

Phæax We are all your Slaves.

Poet. The Joy of all Mankind!

Jewel. Great Spirit of Noblenefs!

Tim.

Tim. We muſt not part this Day, my Friends.

Ap So, ſo, crouching Slaves! Aches contract and make
Your ſupple Joints to wither; that there ſhould be
So little Love among theſe Knaves, yet all this Courteſy!
They hate and ſcorn each other, yet they kiſs
As if they were of different Sexes· Villains! Villains?

Exeunt Omnes.

Enter Evandra. *Re-enter* Timon

Timon. Hail to the fair *Evandra!* methinks your Looks
   are chang'd,
And clouded with ſome Grief that miſbecomes 'em

Evan My Lord, my Ears this Morning were ſaluted with
The moſt unhappy News, the diſmal'ſt Story,
The only one could have afflicted me;
My Dream foretold it, and I wak'd affrighted,
With a cold Sweat o'er all my Limbs.

Tim. What is it, Madam?

Evan. You ſpeak not with the Kindneſs you were wont,
I have been us'd to tenderer Words than theſe.
It is too true, and I am miſerable?

Tim. What is't diſturbs you ſo—too well I gueſs [*Aſide.*

Evan. I hear I am to loſe your Love, which was
The only earthly Bleſſing I enjoy'd,
And that on which my Life depended.

Tim No, I muſt ever love my excellent *Evandra!*

Evan *Meliſſa* will not ſuffer it: Oh cruel *Timon!*
Thou well may'ſt bluſh at thy Ingratitude!
Had I ſo much t'wards thee, I ne'er ſhou'd ſhow
My Face without Confuſion Such a Guilt,
As if I had deſtroy'd thy Race, and ruin'd
All thy Eſtate, and made thee infamous!
Thy Love to me I could prefer before
All cold Reſpects of Kindred, Wealth, and Fame.

Tim You have been kind ſo far above Return,
That 'tis beyond Expreſſion

Evan. Call to Mind
Whoſe Race I ſprung from, that of great *Alcides,*
Tho' not my Fortune, Beauty and my Youth,
And my unſpotted Fame yielded to none.
You on your Knees a thouſand times have ſworn,

That

That they exceeded all, and yet all thefe,
The only Treafures a poor Maid poffeft,
I facrific'd to you, and rather chofe
To throw myfelf away, than you fhould be
Uneafy in your Wifhes; fince which happy,
And yet unhappy Time, you've been to me
My Life, my Joy, my Earth, my Heaven, my All,
I never had one fingle Wifh beyond you;
Nay, every Action, every Thought of mine,
How far foe'er their large Circumference
Stretcht out, yet center'd all in you: You were
My End, the only thing could fill my Mind.

Tim. She ftrikes me to the Heart! I would I had
Not feen her!   [*Afide.*

Evan Ah *Timon!* I have lov'd you fo, that had
My Eyes offended you, I with thefe Fingers
Had pluckt 'em by the Roots, and caft them from me:
Or had my Heart contain'd one Thought that was
Not yours, I with this Hand would rip it open:
Shew me a Wife in *Athens* can fay this;
And yet I am not one, but you are now to marry.

Tim. That I have lov'd you, you and Heav'n can witnefs
By many long repeated Acts of Love
And Bounty I have fhow'd you——

Evan. Bounty! ah *Timon!*
I am not yet fo mean, but I contemn
Your tranfitory Dirt, and all Rewards,
But that of Love; your Perfon was the Bound
Of all my Thoughts and Wifhes; in Return
You *have* lov'd me! Oh miferable Sound!
I would you never had, or always would.

Tim. Man is not Mafter of his Appetites,
Heav'n fways our Mind to Love.

Evan. But Hell to Falfhood:
How many thoufand times y'have vow'd and fworn
Eternal Love; Heav'n has not yet abfolv'd
You of your Oaths to me; nor can I ever,
My Love's as much too much as yours too little.

Tim If you love me, you'll love my Happinefs,
Meliffa; Beauty and her Love to me

Has so inflam'd me, I can have none without her.

   Evan. If I had lov'd another, when you first,
My dear false *Timon*, swore to me, wou'd you
Have wish'd I might have found my Happiness
Within another's Arms . No, no, it is
To Love a Contradiction

   Tim 'Tis a Truth I cannot answer.

   Evan Besides, *Melissa*'s Beauty
Is not believ'd to exceed my little Stock ;
Ev'n Modesty may praise itself when 'tis
Aspers'd But her Love is mercenary,
Most mercenary, base, 'tis Marriage Love :
She gives her Person, but in vile Exchange
She does demand your Liberty But I
Could generously give without mean Bargaining,
I trusted to your Honour, and lost mine,
Lost all my Friends and Kindred ; but little thought
I should have lost my Love, and cast it on
A barren and ungrateful Soil that would return no Fruit.

   Tim This does perplex me, I must break it off [*Aside.*

   Evan The first Storm of your Love did shake me so,
It threw down all my Leaves, my hopeful Blossoms,
Pull'd down my Branches ; but this latter Tempest of your
Strikes at my Root, and I must wither now,   [Hate
Like a desertless, sapless Tree · must fall——

   Tim You are secure against all Injuries
While I have Breath——

   Evan And yet you do the greatest.

   Tim You shall be so much Partner of my Fortune
As will secure you full Respect from all,
And may support your Quality in what Pomp
You can desire.

   Evan. I am not of so coarse a Mold, or have
So gross a Mind, as to partake of aught
That's yours without you——
But oh thou too dear perjur'd Man! I could
With thee prefer a Dungeon, a low and loathsome Dun-
Before the stately gilded fretted Roofs,   [geon!
The Pomp, the Noise, the Show, the Revelling,
And all the glittering Splendor of a Palace.

2

Tim.

Tim. I by refiftlefs Fate am hurry'd on——

Evan A vulgar, mean Excufe for doing ill.

Tim If that were not, my Honour is engag'd——

Evan It had a Pre-engagement——

Tim. All the great Men of *Athens* urge me on
To marry, and to preferve my Race

Evan Suppofe your Wife be falfe (as 'tis not new
In *Athens*) and fuffer others to graft upon
Your Stock, where is your Race? Weak, vulgar Reafon!

Tim Her Honour will not fuffer her

Evan She may do it cunningly, and keep her Honour.

Tim. Her Love will then fecure her, which is as fervent.

Evan As yours was once to me, and may continue
Perhaps as long, and yet you cannot know
She loves you   Since that bafe *Cecropian* Law
Made Love a Merchandife, to traffique Hearts
For Marriage and for Dowry, who's fecure?
Now her great Sign of Love is, fhe's content
To bind you with the ftrongeft Chains, and to
A Slavery nought can manumize you from
But Death   And I could be content to be
A Slave to you, without thofe vile Conditions——

Tim Why are not our Defires within our Power?
Or why fhould we be punifh'd for obeying them?
But we cannot create our own Affections;
They're moved by fome invifible active Pow'r,
And we are only paffive; and whatfoe'er
Of Imperfection follows from th' Obedience
To our Defires, we fuffer, not commit,
And 'tis a cruel and a hard Decree,
That we muft fuffer firft, and then be punifh'd for't.

Evan Your Philofophy is too fubtle——but what
Security of Love from her can be like mine?
Is Marriage a Bond of Truth, which does confift
Of a few trifling Ceremonies? Or are thofe
Charms or Philtres? 'Tis true, my Lord, I was not
Firft lifted o'er the Threfhold, and then
Led by my Parents to *Minerva*'s Temple·
No young unyok'd Heifer's Blood was offer'd
To *Diana*, no Invocation to *Juno* or the *Parcæ:*

No Coachman drove me with a lighted Torch ;
Nor was your Houfe adorn'd with Garlands then ;
Nor had I Figs thrown on my Head, or lighted
By my dear Mother's Torches to your Bed .
Are thefe flight things the Bond of Truth and Conftancy ?
I came all Love into your Arms, unmix'd
With other Aims ; and you for this will caufe
My Death

   Tim I'd fooner feek my own, *Evandra.*

   Evan Ah, my Lord ' if that be true, then go not to
For I fhall die to fee another have   [*Meliffa,*
Poffeffion of all that e'er I wifh'd for on Earth

   Tim. I would I had not feen *Meliffa.*

   Evan. Ah, my dear Lord ' there is fome Comfort left ;
Cherifh thofe noble Thoughts, and they'll grow ftronger,
Your lawful Gratitude and Love will rife,
And quell the other Rebel-Paffion in you.
Ufe all the Endeavours which you can, and if
They fail in my Relief, I'll die to make you happy.

   Tim You have moved me to be womanifh ; pray retire,
I will love you.

   Evan. Oh happy Word ' Heav'n ever blefs my Dear ;
Farewel · But will you never fee *Meliffa* more ?

   Tim Sweet Excellence ' retire.

   Evan I will——will you remember your *Evandra ?*

   Tim Yes, I will.   [*Ex.* Evan.
How happy were Mankind in Conftancy,
Twould equal us with the celeftial Spirits '
O could we meet with the fame Tremblings ftill,
Thofe panting Joys, thofe furious Defires,
Thofe happy Trances which we found at firft ,
But, Oh !

   Unhappy Man, whofe moft tranfporting Joy
   Feeds on fuch lufcious Food as foon will cloy,
   And that which fhould preferve, does it deftroy.
                        [*Exit* Timon.

ACT

ACT II. SCENE I.

Enter Meliſſa *and* Chloe.

Mel. WHAT think'ſt thou, *Chloe?* will this Dreſs become me?

Chl Oh, moſt exceedingly! This pretty Curl does give you ſuch a killing Grace, I ſwear that all the Youth at the Lord *Timon*'s Maſque will die for you.

Mel No: But do'ſt thou think ſo, *Chloe?* I love to make thoſe Fools die for me, and I all the while look ſo ſcornfully, and then, with my Head on one Side, with a languiſhing Eye, I do ſo kill 'em again! Prithee, what do they ſay of me, *Chloe?*

Chl Say! that you are the Queen of all their Hearts, their Goddeſs, their Deſtiny; and talk of *Cupid*'s Flames, and Darts and Wounds! Oh the rareſt Language! 'twould make one die to hear it; and every now and then they ſteal ſome Gold into my Hand, and then commend me too.

Mel Dear Soul, do they? and do they die for me?

Chl Oh yes, the fineſt, propereſt Gentlemen——

Mel But there are not many that die for me? humph---

Chl O yes, *Lamachus, Theodorus, Theſſalus, Eumolpides, Memnon,* and indeed all that ſee your Ladyſhip.

Mel I'll ſwear!—— how is my Complexion to Day? ha, *Chloe?*

Chl O moſt fragrant! 'tis a rare White-waſh this!

Mel. I think it is the beſt I ever bought; had I not beſt lay on ſome more red, *Chloe?*

Chl A little more would do well, it makes you look ſo pretty, and ſo plump, Madam.

Mel. I have been too long this Morning in dreſſing.

Chl. Oh no! I vow you have been but bare three Hours.

Mel No more! well, if I were ſure to be thus pretty but ſeven Years, I'd be content to die on that Condition.

Chl. The Gods forbid.

Mel. I ſwear I would; but do'ſt thou think *Timon* will like me in this Dreſs? Y 2 *Chl.*

Cbl. Oh he dies for you in any Drefs, Madam!

Mel. Oh this vile Taylor, that brought me not home my new Habit To-day; he deferves the Oftracifm! a Villain, to diforder me fo, I am afraid it has done harm to my Complexion. I have dreamt of it thefe two Nights, and fhall not recover it this Week———

Chl. Indeed, Madam, he deferves Death from your Eyes.

Mel. I think I look pretty well will not *Timon* perceive my Diforder?——hah——

Cbl. Oh no; but you fpeak as if you made this killing Preparation for none but *Timon*

Mel. O yes, *Chloe*, for every one; I love to have all the young Blades follow, kifs my Hand, admire, adore me, and die for me But I muft have one favour'd Servant; it is the Game and not the Quarry I muft look after in the reft

Chl. Oh Lord! I would have as many Admirers as I could.

Mel. Ay, fo would I——but favour one alone No, I am refolv'd nothing fhall corrupt my Honefty; thefe Admirers would make one a Whore, *Chloe*, and that undoes us; 'tis our Intereft to be honeft.

Cbl. Would they? No, I warrant you; I'd fain fee any of thefe Admirers make me a Whore.

Mel. *Timon* loves me honeftly, and is rich———

Chl. You have forgot your *Alcibiades*: He is the rareft Perfon!

Mel. No, no, I could love him dearly: Oh! he was the beautiful'ft Man, the fineft Wit in *Athens*; the beft Companion, fulleft of Mirth and Pleafure, and the prettieft Ways he has to pleafe Ladies! He would make his Enemies rejoice to fee him.

Cbl. Why he is all this! and can do all this ftill.

Mel. Ay, but he has been long banifh'd, for breaking *Mercury*'s Images, and profaning the Myfteries of *Proferpine*; befides, the People took his Eftate from him, and I hate a poor Fellow, from my Heart, I fwear, I vow, methinks I look fo pretty To-day, I could kifs myfelf, *Chloe*.

Chl. Oh dear Madam! ——— I could look on you for ever. Oh what a World of Murder you'll commit To-day!

Mel. Doft thou think fo? ha! ha! no, no——

Enter

Enter a Servant

Serv. The Lord *Timon's* come to wait on you, and Begs Admittance.

Enter Timon.

Mel. Defire his Prefence.

Tim. There is Enchantment in her Looks;
Afrefh I am wounded every Time I fee her.
All Happinefs to beautiful *Meliffa*

Mel. I fhall want none in you, my deareft Lord.

Tim. Sweeteft of Creatures, in whom all th' Excellence
Of heav'nly Woman kind is feen unmixt;
Nature has wrought thy Metal up without Allay.

Mel. I have no Value, but my Love of you,
And that I am fure has no Allay, 'tis of
So ftrong a Temper, neither Time, nor Death,
Nor any Change can break it——

Tim. Dear charming Sweet, thy Value is fo great,
No Kingdom upon Earth fhould buy thee from me :
But I have ftill an Enemy with you,
That guards me from my Happinefs; a Vow
Againft the Law of Nature, againft Love,
The beft of Nature, and the higheft Law.

Mel. It will be but a Week in Force.

Tim. 'Tis a whole Age: In all approaching Joys,
The nearer they come to us, ftill the Time
Seems longer to us : But my dear *Meliffa*,
Why fhould we bind our felves with Vows and Oaths ?
Alas ! by Nature we are too much confin'd ;
Our Liberty's fo narrow, that we need not
Find Fetters for our felves : No, we fhould feize
On Pleafure wherefoever we find it,
Left at another Time we mifs it there.

Chl. Madam, break your Vow, it was a rafh one.

Mel. Thou foolifh Wench ! I cannot get my Things
In Order till that Time ? do'ft think I will
Be marry'd like fome vulgar Creature, which
Snatches at the firft Offer, as if fhe
Were defperate of having any other ?

Tim. Is there no Hope that you will break your Vow ?

Mel. If any Thing, one Word of yours wou'd do't.

But

But how can you be once fecure I'll keep
A Vow to you, that would not to myfelf?

Tim. Some dreadful Accident may come, *Meliffa,*
To interrupt our Joys, let us make fure
O'th' prefent Minute, for the reft, perhaps,
May not be ours.

Mel. It is not fit it fhou'd, if I fhou'd break a Vow;
No, you fhall never find a Change in me,
All the fix'd Stars fhall fooner ftray
With an irregular Motion, than I change:
This may affure you of my Love, if not,
Upon my Knees I fwear————
Were I the Queen of all the Univerfe,
And *Timon* were reduc'd to Rags and Mifery,
I would not change my Love to him.

Tim. And here I Vow,
Should all the Frame of Nature be diffolv'd,
Should the firm Center fhake, fhould Earthquakes rage
With fuch a Fury to diforder all
The peaceful and agreeing Elements,
Till they were huddled into their firft *Chaos,*
As long as I could be, I'd be the fame,
The fame Adorer of *Meliffa!*

Mel. This is fo great a Bleffing Heav'n can't add to it.

Tim. Thou art my Heav'n, *Meliffa,* the laft Mark
Of all my Hopes and Wifhes, fo I prize thee,
That I could die for thee

    Enter a Servant of Timon's.

Serv. My Lord, your Dinner's ready, and your Lordfhip's Guefts wait your wifh'd-for Prefence: The Lord
Nicias is a'ready there

Tim. Let's hafte to wait on him, *Meliffa*

Mel. It is my Duty to my Father   [*Exeunt.*

Enter Poet, Apemantus, Servants *fetting Things in Order
for the Feaft-*

Poet. His Honour will foon be here, I have prepar'd
the Mafkers; they are ready.

Apem. How now, *Poet!* what Piece of Foppery haft
thou to prefent to *Timon?*

            Poet.

Poet. Thou art a fenfelefs, fnarling *Stoick,* and haft no Tafte of Poetry.

Apem. Thy Poetry's infipid, none can tafte it:
Thou art a wordy, foolifh Scribler, who
Writ'ft nothing but high-founding, frothy Stuff;
Thou fpread'ft, and beat'ft out thy poor little Senfe;
'T is all Leaf-Gold, it has no Weight in it.
Thou lov'ft impertinent Defcription,
And when thou haft a Rapture, it is not
The facred Rapture of a Poet, but
Incoherent, extravagant, and unnatural,
Like mad Mens Thoughts; and this thou call'ft poetical.

Poet. You a Judge! fhall dull Philofophers judge
Of us, the nimble Fancies and quick Spirits
Of th' Age?

Apem. The Coxcombs of the Age! Are there fuch eminent Fopperies as in the Poets of this Time? Their moft unreafonable Heads are whimfical, and fantaftick as Fidlers. They are the Scorn and Laughter of all witty Men; The Folly of you makes the Art contemptible: None of you have the Judgment of a Gander.

Enter Ælius, Nicias, Phæax, and the other Senators

Poet. You are a bafe, fnarling Critick; write yourfelf, and you dare.

Apem I confefs 'tis a daring Piece of Valour, for a Man of Senfe, to write to an Age that likes your fpurious Stuff

Nic. What Time of the Day is't, *Apemantus?*

Apem Time to be honeft.

Ælius. That Time ferves always.

Apem. Then what Excufe haft thou, that would'ft thus long omit it?

Ifid. You ftay to be at the Lord *Timon's* Feaft?

Apem. Yes, to fee Meat fill Knaves, and Wine heat Fools.

Cleon. Well, fare thee well

Apem. Thou art an Afs to bid me farewel.

Cleon. Why fo?

Apem. Becaufe I have not fo little Reafon or Honefty to return thee one good Wifh for it.

Phæax.

Phæax Go hang thyfelf!

Apem I'll do nothing at thy bidding, make thy Requefts to thy Friend, if there be fuch a Wretch on Earth

Phæax Be gone, unpeaceable Dog! or I will fpurn thee from me

Apem Tho' I am none, I'll fly like a Dog at the Heels of the Afs

Nic He's oppofite to all Humanity——

Ælius Now we fhall tafte of *Timon*'s Bounty

Phæax He has a Heart brimful of Kindnefs and Good-will——

Ifid And pours it down on all his Friends, as if *Plutus*, the God of Wealth, were but his Steward.

Phæax No Meed but he repays fev'n-fold above its felf, no Gift but breeds the Giver fuch Return as does exceed his Wifhes.

Thrafil He bears the noblest Mind that ever govern'd Man

Phæax Long may he live with profperous Fortunes. But I fear it——

Ælius I hear a Whifper, as though he fails his Creditors, even of their Intereft

Phæax I fear it is too true—well, 'tis Pity: But he's a good Lord!

Enter Timon *with* Meliffa, Chloe, Nicias, *and a great Train with him.*

Here he comes——My Noble Lord!

Nic. Moft worthy *Timon*!

Ælius My moft honoured Lord!

Tim You over-joy me with your Prefence! is there on Earth a Sight fo fplendid, as Tables well fill'd with good and faithful Friends, like you—Dear *Meliffa*! be pleas'd to know my Friends—Oh *Apemantus*! thou'rt welcome.

Apem No, thou fhalt not make me welcome;
I come to tell thee Truth, and if thou hear'ft me,
I'll lock thy Heav'n from thee hereafter. Think
On the Edd of your Eftate, and Flow of Debts;
How many prodigal Bits do Slaves and Flatterers gorge?
And now 'tis noble *Timon*! worthy *Timon*! royal *Timon*!
And when the Means is gone that buys this Praife,

The

The Breath is gone whereof the Praife is made.

Tim. It is not fo with my Eftate

Apem. None are fo honeft to tell thee of thy Vanities,
So the Gods blefs me.
When all your Offices have been oppreft
With riotous Feeders, when every Vault has wept
With drunken Spilth of Wine, when every Room
Has blaz'd with Lights, and bray'd with Minftrels,
Or roaring finging Drunkards ; I have retir'd
To my poor homely Cell, and fet my Eyes
At flow for thee, becaufe I find fomething
In thee that might be worthy——but as thou art,
I hate and fcorn thee.

Tim Come, preach no more, had I no Eftate, I
Am rich in Friends, my noble Friends here,
The deareft, loving Friends that ever Man
Was bleft with.

Nic. Oh might we have
An happy Opportunity to fhew
How we love and honour you !

Ælius. That you wou'd once but ufe our Hearts.

Ifand We'd lay 'em out all in your Service.

Phæax Yes, all ourfelves, if you would put us to
A Tryal, then we were perfect

Tim I doubt it not, I know you'd ferve me all:
Shall I diftruft my Friends ? I have often wifht
My felf poorer, that I might ufe you——We are
Born to do good one to another : Friends,
Unlefs we ufe 'em, are like fweet Inftruments
Hung up in Cafes But oh, what a precious Comfort
'Tis to have fo many like Brothers, commanding
One another's Fortunes ! Truft me, my Joy brings Water
To my Eyes

Phæax Joy had the like Conception in my Eyes.

Apem Ho, ho, ho——I laugh to think that it con-
ceiv'd a Baftard.

Tim What doft thou laugh for ?

Apem. To hear thefe Smell-feafts lie and fawn fo, not
only flattering thee, but thy Mutton and thy Partridge ·

} Thefe

Thefe Flies, who at one Cloud of Winter-fhowers would drop from off you.

Cleon Silence the Dog !

Phæax Let the fnarling Cur be kickt out.

Apem Of what vile Earth, of what mean Dirt, a Lord is kneaded !

Tim The Man I think is honeft, and his Humour hurts us not.

Apem I would my Reafon wou'd do thee good, *Timon.*

Mel. This is an odd fnarling Fellow; I like him.

Apem If I could, without lying, I'd fay the fame of thee.

Mel Why prithee what doft think of me?

Tim. He'll fnarle at thee

Mel No Matter

Apem I think thou art a Piece of white and red Earth, the Picture of Vanity drawn to the Life; I am thinking how handfome that Skull will be when all the Flefh is off: That Face thou art fo proud of is a poor, vain, tranfitory Thing, and fhortly will be good for nothing

Mel Out on him ! fcurvy poor Fellow!

Tim No more of this, be not fo fullen, I'll be kind to thee, and better thy Condition

Apem No, I'll have nothing; fhould I be brib'd too, there would be none left to rail at thee, and then thoud'ft fin the fafter : *Timon,* thou giveft fo long, thou'lt fhortly give thyfelf away.

Tim I'll hear no more ; let him have a Table by himfelf.

Apem. Let me have fome Roots and Water, fuch as Nature intended for our Meat and Drink, before Eating and Drinking grew into an Art

[*The Meat is ferv'd up with Kettle-Drums and Trumpets.*

Tim. Sit, dear *Meliffa,* this is your Feaft,
All you fee is yours ;
And all that you can wifh for fhall be fo.
Come, fit, Lords, no Ceremony,
That was devis'd at firft to fet a Glofs
On feigned Deeds, and hollow-hearted Welcomes;
Recanting Goodnefs, forry ere 'tis fhewn
True Friendfhip needs 'em not; you're more welcome

To

To my Fortunes than my Fortunes are to me. [*They fit*
Will you not have some Meat, *Apemantus?*

Apem. I scorn thy Meat, 'twould choak me; for I should
Ne'er flatter ye. Ye Gods, what a Number of Men
Eat *Timon!* and yet he sees 'em not
It grieves me to see so many dip their Meat
In one Man's Blood; and all the Madness is,
He cheers 'em to't, and loves 'em for't.
I wonder Men dare trust themselves with Men:
Methinks they should invite them without Knives,
'Twere safer far   That Fellow that sits next him,
Now parts Bread with him, pledges his Breath
In a divided Draught, may next Day kill him.
Such things have been   If I were a Huge Man,
I should b' afraid to drink at Meals,
Lest they should spy my Windpipe's dangerous Places:
Great Men should drink with Harness on their Throats.

Tim Now, my Lords, let *Melissa*'s Health go round.

Ælius. Let it flow this Way.

[*Kettle Drums and Trumpets sound.*

Apem How this Pomp shews to a little Oil and Roots'
——These Healths will make thee and thy State look ill.

Phæax. Here's that which is too weak to be a Sinner;
Here's honest Water ne'er left Man i'th' Mire,
This and my Root will still keep down
My saucy and presumptuous Flesh,
That it shall never get the better of me——

Apemantus's Grace.
Immortal Gods, I crave no Pelf,
I pray for no Man but my self.
Grant, I may never be so fond
To trust Man on his Oath or Bond;
Or a Harlot for her weeping,
Or a Dog that seems a sleeping;
Or a Goaler with my Freedom,
Or my Friends, if I should need 'em.
Amen, Amen, and so fall to't;
Great Men sin, and I eat Root.

Much Good may't do thee, good *Apemantus.*

Z

Nic Our noble Lord *Timon*'s Health, let it go round,
And Drums and Trumpets found   [*Kettle-Drums, &c*
  Apem What Madnefs is the Pomp, the Noife, the
      Splendor,
The frantick Glory of this foolifh Life !
Ve make our felves Fools to difport our felves,
And vary a Thoufand antick ugly Shapes
Of Folly and of Madnefs; thefe fill up
The Scenes and empty Spaces of our Lives.
Life's nothing but a dull Repetition,
\ vain fantaftick Dream, and there's an End on't
  Tim Now, my good Lords and Friends, I fpeak to you,
ou that are of the Council of Four Hundred,
· the Behalf of a dear Friend of mine.
  Nic One Word of yours muft govern all the Council,
ad any thing in *Athens*
  Tim I fpeak chiefly
ɔ you, my Lord and Father, and to *Phæax.*
  Phæax My good Lord, command me to my Death,
l I'll obey.
  Tim I have receiv'd Notice from *Alcibiades*
Thofe Enemies you've been, and whofe Friends
beg you will be now) that he in private
'ill venture into *Athens* ,
ot openly, becaufe he will not truft
he Infolence of the tumultuous Rabble ;
  he follicites his Recalment with you,
here lives not on this Earth a Man that has
eferv'd fo well from the Nobility ;
Ie has preferv'd ev'n *Athens* in his Exile.
By *Tiffaphernes'* Pow'r he has kept us from
The *Lacedæmonian* Rage¡ and other Foes,
¯hat might have laid this City low in Afhes
Iow many famous Battles has he won ?
¡ut which is more, by his Advice and Power,
ɔ̈ven in his Abfence, he has wrefted
he Government from the infulting Vulgar,
Ṽhofe Wifdom's Blindnefs, and whofe Pow'r is Madnefs,
ʼnd plac'd it in your noble Hands , methinks
'ou, in Return, fhould take off his hard Sentence   Of

Of Banifhment, and render back all his Eftate.

Phæax Is there a thing on Earth you would command us
That we would difobey?

Nic I am abfolutely yours in all Commands.

Æhus How proud am I, that I can ferve Lord *Timo.*

Apem Think'ft thou thyfelf thy Country's Friend, nov
His foul Riot, and his inordinate Luft, [*Timon!*
His wavering Paffions, and his headlong Will,
His felfifh Principles, his Contempt of others,
His Mockery, his various Sports, his Wantonnefs,
The Rage and Madnefs of his Luxury,
Will make th' *Athenians* Heart ake, as thy own
Will foon make thine.

Ifid Hang him, we never mind him.

Ifand When will he fpeak well of any Man?

Apem When I can find a Man that's better than
A Beaft, I will fall down, and worfhip him.

Tim. Thou art an *Athenian*, and I bear with thee.
Is the Mafque ready?

Poet. 'Tis, my noble Lord

Apem. What odd and childifh Folly Slaves find out,
To pleafe and court all thy diftemper'd Appetites!
They fpend their Flatteries to devour thofe Men
Upon whofe Age they'll void it up again
With poifonous Spite and Envy.
Who lives that's not deprav'd, or elfe depraves?
Who die that bear not fome Spurns to their Graves
Of their Friends giving? I fhould fear that thofe
Who now are going to dance before me,
Should one Day ftamp on me. It has been done.

Tim Nay, if you rail at all Society,
I'll hear no more—begone.

Apem Thou may'ft be fure I will not ftay to fee
Thy Folly any longer, fare thee well, remember
Thou would'ft not hear me, thou wilt curfe thyfelf for't.

Tim. I do not think fo—fare thee well. [*Ex* Apem.

Enter Servant.

Serv. My Lord, there are fome Ladies mafk'd defire
Admittance

Tim. Have not my Doors been always open to

Ever'

Every *Athenian?* They do me Honour,
Wait on 'em in, were I not bound to do
My Duty here, I would

Chloe. I have not had the Opportunity
To deliver this till now, it is a Letter
From *Alcibiades.*

Mel. Dear *Alcibiades!* How I shall love him,
When he's restor'd to his Estate and Country !
He will be richer far than *Timon* is,
And I shall chuse him first of any Man ;
How lucky 'tis I should put off my Wedding !

    Enter Evandra *with Ladies mask'd*

Tim Ladies, you do my House and me great Honour,
I should be glad you would unmask, that I
Might see to whom I owe the Obligation.

1 *Lady* We ask your Pardon, we are stoln out upon
Curiosity, and dare not own it

Tim Your Pleasure, Ladies, shall be mine

Evan This is the fine gay Thing so much admir'd,
That's born to rob me of my Happiness,
And of my Life , her Face is not her own,
Nor is her Love, nor Speech, nor Motion so:
Her Smiles, her amorous Looks, she puts on all,
There's nothing natural : She always acts,
And never shews herself ; how blind is Love
That cannot see this Vanity ! [*Masque begins.*

    Enter Shepherds *and* Nymphs.

A Symphony of Pipes imitating the chirping of Birds.

Nymph *Hark how the Songsters of the Grove*
   Sing Anthems to the God of Love
   Hark how each am'rous winged Pair
   With Love's great Praises fill the Air.

Chorus *On ev'ry Side the charming Sound*
   Does from the hollow Woods rebound

           Retornella.

N,mph. *Love in their little Veins inspires*
   Their chearful Notes, their soft Desires
   While Heat makes Buds or Blossoms spring,
   Those pretty Couples love and sing

           Chorus

Chorus with Flutes.
But Winter puts out their Desire,
And half the Year they want Love's Fire.

Retornella

Full Chorus.
But ah how much are our Delights more dear !
For only Human-kind love all the Year.

Enter the *Mænades* and *Ægipanes.*

1 Bacch. *Hence with your trifling Deity,*
   A greater we adore ,
  Bacchus, *who always kept us free*
   From that blind childish Pow'r.

2 Bacch. *Love makes you languish, and look pale,*
   And sneak, and sigh, and whine ,
  But over us no Griefs prevail,
   While we have lusty Wine

Chorus with Hautboys
Then hang the dull Wretch who has Care in his Soul,
Whom Love, or whom Tyrants, or Laws can controul,
If within his right Hand he can have a full Bowl.

Nymph 1.
Go drivel and snore with your fat God of Wine,
 Your swell'd Faces with Pimples adorning ;
Soak your Brains over-night, and your Senses resign,
 And forget all you did the next Morning.

Nymph 2
With dull aching Noddles live long in a Mist,
 And never discover true Joy ·
Would Love tempt with Beauty, you could not resist,
 The Empire he slights' he'd destroy

1 Bacch. *Better our Heads than Hearts should ache,*
   His childish Empire we despise ;
  Good Wine a Slave of him can make,
   And force a Lover to be wise
  Better, &c.

2 Bacch *Wine sweetens all the Cares of Peace,*
   And takes the Terror off from War ;
  To Love's Affliction it gives Ease,
   And to its Joy does best prepare.
  It sweetens, &c

Z 3

Nymph

Nymph.   '*Tis Love that makes great Monarchs fight,*
　　　　　　The End of Wealth and Pow'r is Love ;
　　　　　　It makes the youthful Poets write,
　　　　　　And does the old to Youth improve.
　　　　　　　　　　　　　　　Retornella of Hautboys.

Bacch.   '*Tis Wine that revels in their Veins,*
　　　　　　Makes Cowards vahant, Fools grow wise,
　　　　　　Provokes low Pens to lofty Strains,
　　　　　　And makes the young Love's Chains despise.
　　　　　　　　　　　　　　　　　　Retornella.

Nymphs *and* Shepherds.　*Love rules the World.*
Mænades *and* Ægipanes　'*Tis Wine, 'tis Wine*
Nymphs *and* Shepherds.　'*Tis Love, 'tis Love.*
Mænades *and* Ægipanes.　'*Tis Wine, 'tis Wine.*
　　　　　　　Enter Bacchus *and* Cupid
Bacchus.   *Hold, hold, our Forces are combin'd,*
　　　　　　And we together rule Mankind.
　　　　　　　　　General Chorus
Then we with our Pipes and our Voices will join,
To sound the loud Praises of Love and good Wine.
Wine gives Vigour to Love, Love makes Wine go down,
And by Love and good Drinking all the World is our own.

Tim   'Tis well defign'd, and well perform'd, and I'll reward you well · Let us retire into my next Apartment, where I've devis'd new Pleasures for you, and where I will diftribute fome fmall Prefents, to teftify my Love and Gratitude

Phæax   A Noble Lord!

Ælius   Bounty itfelf!

Tim.   Thus, my *Melissa*, will we always spend Our Time in Pleafures, but whoe'er enjoys thee, Has all this Life affords fumm'd up in that

Evar.   Thefe Words did once belong to me, but oh! My ftubborn Heart, wilt thou not break at this?

Tim.   Ladies, I hope you'll honour me with your Prefence, and accept of a Collation

ı Lady.   We afk your Pardon, and muft leave you.

Tim   *Demetrius*, wait on them.

Evan   My Lord, I'd fpeak with you alone.

　　　　　　　　　　　　　　　　　Tim.

Tim Be pleafed, Madam, to retire with your Father,
I'll wait on you inftantly.   *(To* Melifla.

    [*Exeunt all but* Timon *and* Evandra.

Who are you, Madam ?

  Evan One who is come to take her laft Leave of you.

  Tim. Evandra ! What Confufion am I in !

  Evan. I am forry, in the Midft of all your Joys,
I fhould difturb you thus · I had a Mind
To fee you once before I dy'd ; I ne'er
Shall trouble you again.

  Tim. Let me not hear thefe killing Words.

  Evan. They'll be my laft, and therefore give 'em room :
I'm haft'ning to my Death, then you'll be happy,
I ne'er fhall interrupt your Joys again,
Unlefs the Memory of me fhould make
You drop fome Tears upon my Duft ; I know
Your noble Nature will remember that
Evandra was, and once was dear to you,
And lov'd you fo, that fhe could die to make
You happy.

  Tim. Ah dear *Evandra !* that would make
Me wretched far below all Mifery ,
I'd rather kill myfelf than hear that News :
I call the Gods to witnefs, there's not one
On Earth I more efteem

  Evan. Efteem ! alas !
It is too weak a Cordial to preferve
My fading Life ; I fee your Paffion's grown
Too headftrong for you   Oh my deareft *Timon !*
I, while I have any Breath, muft call you fo ;
Had you once ftruggled for my Sake,
And ftriven to oppofe the raging Fury of
Your fatal Love, I fhould have dy'd contented.
But oh ! falfe to your felf, to all my Hopes,
And me ; you fuck'd the fubtile Poifon in
So greedily, you would not ftay to tafte it.

  Tim. She moves me ftrongly ; I have found from her
The trueft and the tendereft Love that e'er
Woman yet bore to Man.

  Evan. I find you're gone too far in the Difeafe

T

T' admit a Cure: I will perfuade no longer;
Death is my Remedy, and I'll embrace it.

Tim Oh! talk not of Death; I'll love you ftill:
I can love two at once, truft me, I can

Evan No, *Timon,* I will have you whole or nothing:
I love you fo, I cannot live to fee
That dear, that moft ador'd Perfon in another's Arms.
My Love's too nice, 'twill not be fed with Crumbs,
And broken Meat, that falls from your *Meliffa*
No, dear, falfe Man, you foon fhall be at reft,
I came but to receive a parting Kifs,
You'll not deny me that!

Tim I'll not part with you, we'll be Friends for ever.

Evan No, no, it cannot be; forgive this Trouble,
Since 'tis the laft, I'll never fee you more,
And may *Meliffa* ever love you as
The Excellence of your Form deferves; and may
She pleafe you longer than th' unfortunate
Evandra could.

Tim Gods! Why fhould I not love this Woman beft?
She has deferv'd beyond all Meafure from me,
She's beautiful, and good as Angels are,
But I have had her Love already
Oh moft accurfed Charm, that thus prevents me! [*Afide.*
You've made a Woman of me   [*To her.*

Evan I'll have but one laft Look of that
Bewitching Face that ruin'd me
Oh! I could devour it with my Eyes, but I'll
Remove them from thee   I ne'er
Shall die contented while I look on thee.

Tim Be patient, till I give thee Satisfaction

Evan No, deareft Enemy, I'll remove the Guilt
From thee, and thus I'll place it on myfelf
                              [*Offers to ftab herfelf*

Tim Hold, dear *Evandra,* if thou lov'ft my Life,
Preferve thy own, for here I fwear, that Minute
When thou attemp'ft thy Life, I will lofe mine.
Where's *Diphilus?*

            Enter Diphilus.
Diph. Here, my Lord.

                                        Timon.

Tim. Wait on *Evandra* home, and take you Care
Sh' attempts not any Mischief on herself
She's agitated by a dang'rous Passion.——
My Dear let *Diphilus* wait on thee home;
As soon as e'er my Company is gone,
I'll see thee, and convince thee that I love thee
   Evan. No, no; I cannot hope——farewel for ever.
                      [*Ex.* Diph. *and* Evan.

   Tim. I must resolve on something for her Comfort;
For the Empire of the Earth I would not lose her;
There is not one of all her Sex exceeds her
In Love or Beauty———
O miserable State of human Life!
We slight all the Enjoyments which we have,
And those things only value which we have not:
Where is *Demetrius?*
   Dem My Lord!
   Tim. Where is the Casket which I spoke for?
   Dem It is here, my Lord, I beg your Lordship hear me
I have Business that concerns you nearly——   [speak;
   Tim Some other time; of late thou do'st perplex me
Each Moment with the hateful Name of Business,
That mortal Foe to Pleasure; I'll not hear it.   [*Ex.* Tim.
   Dem So! all now is at an End!
He does command us to provide great Gifts,
And all out of an empty Coffer
His Promises fly so beyond his 'Store,
That what he speaks is all in Debt; he owes
For every Word; his Land is all engag'd,
His Money gone; would I were gently turn'd
Out of my Office, lest he should borrow all
I've gotten in his Service. Well!
   Happier is he that has no Friend to feed,
   Than such who do e'en Enemies exceed.   [*Exit.*

                            A C T

ACT III. SCENE I.

Enter Timon *and* Demetrius.

Tim. DEmetrius!
How comes it that I have been thus encounter'd
With clamorous Demands of broken Bonds,
And the unjust Detention of Money long since due?
I knew I was in Debt, but did not think
I had gone so far, wherefore before this Time
Did you not lay my State fully before me,

Dem You would not hear me
At many Times I brought in my Accounts,
Laid 'em before you——you would throw 'em off,
And say, you found 'em in my Honesty.
I have, beyond good Manners, pray'd you often
To hold your Hand more close, and was rebuk'd for't.

Tim You should have prest it further.

Dem Whate'er I durst I did, it was my Interest;
For if my Lord be poor, what then must I be?
Call me before the exactest Auditors,
And let my Life lie on the Proof·
Oh! my good Lord, the World is but a World!
If it were your's to give it at a Breath,
How quickly were it gone?

Tim Have you no Money in the Treasury?

Dem Not enough to supply the Riot of two Meals.

Tim Let all my Land be sold.

Dem 'Tis all engag'd,—
And some already's forfeited and gone;
That which remains will scarce pay present Dues;
The future comes apace

Tim. To *Lacædemon* did my Lands extend.

Dem.

Dem. How many Times have I retir'd and wept,
To think what it would come to.

Tim Prithee, no more! I know thou'rt honeft

Dem It grieves me to confider 'mongft what Parafites
And Trencher-Friends your Wealth has been divided.
I cannot but weep at the fad Reflect on,
When every Word of theirs was greedily
Attended to, as if they'd been pronounc'd
From Oracles, I never could be heard.

Tim. Come, preach no more; thou foon fhalt find that I
Have not mifplac'd my Bounty.   Why doft weep ?
I'm rich in Friends, and can ufe their Wealth
Freely, as I can bid thee fpeak.

Dem I doubt it.

Tim You foon fhall fee how you miftake my Fortune.
Now I fhall try my Friends   Who waits there ?
                    Enter three Servants.

1 *Ser.* My Lord!

Tim Go you to *Phæax* and to *Cleon*; you to *Ifander*
And *Ælius*; you to *Ifidore* and *Thrafillus.*
Commend me to their Loves, and let them know,
I'm proud that my Occafions make me ufe 'em
For a Supply of Money   Let the Requeft
Be fifty Talents from each Man.

1 *Ser.* We will, my Lord.

Tim. Thou, *Demetrius*, fhalt go to the Senate, from
Even to the State's beft Health, I have deferv'd   [whom
This Hearing · Petition them to fend me 500 Talents.

Dem I muft obey! The next Room's full of importa-
nate Slaves and hungry Creditors, go not to 'em
                                [*Ex* Dem.

Tim What! muft my Doors b'oppos'd againft my Paf-
Have I been ever free, and thofe been open   [fage?
For all *Athemans* to go in and out
At their own Pleafure! My Porter at my Gate
Ne'er kept Man out! but fmil'd, and did invite
All that paft by it in, and muft he be
My Goaler, and my Houfe my Prifon! no
I'll not defpair, my Friends will never fail me   [*Exit*

SCENE

SCENE *is the Porch or Cloyster of the* Stoicks.

Apemantus, *speaking to the People and several Senators*

Apem. 'Mongst all the loathsome and base Diseases of
Corrupted Nature, Pride is most contagious.
Behold the poorest miserable Wretch
Which the Sun shines on, in the midst of all
Diseases, Rags, Want, Infamy, and Slavery,
The Fool will find out something to be proud of.

Ælius This is all railing
                                                              ['em:
Apem When you deserve my Precepts, you shall have
Mean while, if I'll be honest, I must rail at you

Cleon Let's walk, hang him, hear him not rail

Phæax Our Government is too remiss in suffering the
Licence of Philosophers, Orators, and Poets

Apem. Show me a mighty Lordling, who's puft up,
And swells with the Opinion of his Greatness;
He's an Ass, for why does he respect himself so,
But to make others do it? wretcled Ass!
By the same means he seeks Respect, he loses it.
Mean Thing! does he not play the Fool, and eat,
And drink, and void his Excrements, and stink,
Like other Men? and die and rot so too?
What then should it be proud of? 'Tis a Load!
And that's a Word some other Men cannot
Prefix before their Names What then? A Word
That it was born to, and then it could not help it,
Or if 'twas made a Lord, perhaps it was
                         Enter Timon's *three Servants*
By Blindness or Partiality i'th Government
If for Desert, he loses it in Pride,
Whoever's proud of his good Deeds, performs
Them for himself, himself should then reward 'em.
Oh! but perhaps he's rich! 'Tis a Million to one
There was Villany in the getting of that Dirt.
And he has the Nobility to have
Knaves for his Ancestors

Phæax Hang thee, thou snarling Rascal! The Government's to blame in suffering thee to rail so long.

Apem. The Government's to blame in suffering the Things I rail at, in suffering Judges without Beards, or Law; Secretaries that can't write; Generals that durst not fight, Ambassadors that can't speak Sense; Blockheads to be great Ministers, and Lord it over witty Men; suffering great Men to sell their Country for filthy Bribes; old limping Senators to sell their Souls for vile Extortion, Matrons to turn incontinent, and Magistrates to pimp for their own Daughters Ruin of Orphans, Treachery, Murther, Rapes, Incests, Adulteries, and unnatural Sins fill all your Dwellings Here's the Shame of Government, and not my Railing. Men of harden'd Foreheads, and fear'd Hearts 'Tis a weak and infirm Government, that is so froward it cannot beat Mens Words

Ælius. Well, babbling philosophical Rascal! we shall make you tremble one Day.

Apem Never.
Sordid great Man! it is not in your Power.
I fear not Man, no more than I can love him:
'Twere better for us that wild Beasts possest
The Empire of the Earth, they'd use Men better
Than they do one another: They'd ne'er prey
On Man but for Necessity of Nature.
Man undoes Man, in Wantonness and Sport,
Brutes are much honester than he, my Dog,
When he fawns on me, is no Courtier,
He is in earnest; but a Man shall smile,
And wish my Throat cut

Cleon. Money of me; say'st thou?

1 *Ser* Yes! he says he's proud he has Occasion to make use of you.

Cleon. Is't come to that? [*Aside.*
Unfortunate Man! I have not half a Talent by me! But here are other Lords can do it. I honour him so, that if he will, I'll sell my Land for him; but prithee excuse me to him; I am in great Haste at this Time [*Ex* Cleon.

1 *Ser.* 'Tis as I thought! How most'rous and deform'd a Thing is base Ingratitude! Here's *Phæax.* ——— My Lord!

Phæax. Oh! one of Lord *Timon's* Men! a Gift, I
warrant

warrant you   Why this hits right   I dreamt of a Silver
Bafon and Ewer to Night! How does that honourable,
compleat, free-hearted Gentleman, the very bountiful
good Lord?

    1 *Ser* Well in his Health, my Lord

    Phæax I am heartily glad , what haft thou under thy
Cloak, honeft Youth?

    1 *Ser* An empty Box, which, by my Lord's Com-
mand, I come to entreat your Honour to fupply with fifty
Talents he has inftant Need of. He bid me fay, he does
not doubt your Friendfhip

    Phæax Hum! not doubt it! alas, good Lord! He's a
noble Gentleman! had he not kept fo good a Houfe,
'would have been better , I've often din'd with him, and
told him of it, and come again to Supper, for that Pur-
pofe, to have him fpend lefs, but 'twould not do ; I am
forry for't But, good Lad! thou art hopeful, and of
good Parts!

    1 *Ser* Your Lordfhip fpeaks your Pleafure

    Phæax A prompt Spirit to give thee thy due. Thou
know'ft what's Reafon, and can'ft ufe thy Time well, if
the Time ufe thee well ——'Tis no Time to lend Money
Thou art wife , here's Money for thee———Good Lad,
wink at me, and fay, thou faw'ft me not.

    1 *Ser* Is't poffible the World fhould differ fo,
And we alive that liv'd in't?

    Apem What! art thou fent to invite thofe Knaves a-
gain to feaft with thy luxurious Lord?

    1 *Ser* No· I came to borrow fifty Talents for him ;
and this Lord has given me this to fay, I did not fee him.

    Apem Is't come to that already?
Bafe, flavifh *Phæax*! thou of the Nobility!
Let molten Coin be thy Damnation

    Phæax Peace, Dog!

    Apem Thou Worm! thou Trencher-Fly! thou Flatterer!
Thou haft *Timon*'s Meat ftill in thy gluttonous Paunch,
And do'ft deny him Money. Why fhould it thrive,
And turn to Nutriment, when thou art Poifon!

    2 *Ser* My noble Lord!

    Lland. Oh how does thy brave Lord, my nobleft Friend?
                                                    2 *Ser.*

2 *Ser* May it pleafe your Honour, he has fent———

Ifand Hay ——— what has he fent? I am fo much oblig'd to him, he's ever fending How fhall I thank him ? hah ! What has he fent ?

2 *Ser* He has fent me to tell you, he has Occafion to ufe your Friendfhip, he has inftant need of fifty Talents-–-

Ifand Is that your Bufinefs? hah !
I know his Honour is but merry with me,
He cannot want as many Hundreds

2 *Ser* Yes, he wants fifty, but is affur'd of your Honour's Friendfhip

Ifand Thou art not fure in Earneft !

2 *Ser.* Upon my Life I am

Ifand What an unfortunate Wretch am I ? to disfurnifh Myfelf upon fo good a Time,
When I might have fhewn how much I love
And honour him . This is the greateft Affliction
E'er fell upon me ! The Gods can witnefs for me.
I was juft fending to my Lord myfelf
I have no Power to ferve him, my Heart bleeds for't:
I hope his Honour will conceive the beft,
Beaft that I am ! that the firft good Occafion
Shou'd not be in my Power to ufe ! I beg .
A thoufand Pardons———Tell him fo———

Apem: Thou art an excellent Summer-Friend !
How often haft thou dipt i'th' Difh with him ?
He has been a Father to thee, with his Purfe
Supported thy Eftate , whene'er thou drink'ft,
His Silver kiffes thy bafe Lips , thou rid'ft upon
His Horfes, ly'ft on his Beds

Ifand. Peace, or I'll knock thy Brains out. [*Ex.* Ifand.

3 *Ser.* My Lord *Thrafillus*———

Thraf He's come to borrow, I muft fhun him. [*Afide.*
I hope my Lord is well.

3 *Ser.* Yes, my Lord, and has fent me———

Thraf To invite me to Dinner. I am in great Hafte—
But I'll wait on him if I can poffibly   [*Ex.* Thraf.

Apem. Good Fool go home. Doft think to find a grateful Man in *Athens* ?

3 *Ser.* If my Lord's Occafions did not prefs him

very much, I would not urge it.

Ælius Why wou'd he send to me ? I am poor; there's *Phæax, Clean, Isidore, Thrasillus,* and *Isander,* and many Men that owe their Fortunes to him.

3 *Ser* They have been touch'd, and found base Metal

Ælius Have they deny'd him, and must you come to Must I be his last Refuge ? 'tis a great Slight, [me ? Must I be the last sought to ? he might have Consider'd who I am

3 *Ser* I see he did not know you

Ælius I was the first that e'er receiv'd Gift from him, And I will keep it for his Honour's sake ; But at present I cannot possibly supply him : Besides, my Father made me sware, upon His Death, I never should lend Mony. I've kept the Oath e'er since. Fare thee well. [*Exit* Ælius.

3 *Ser* They all fly us !

Apem The barbarous Herd of Mankind shun One in Affliction, and turn him out, As Deer do one that's hunted —— Go, go home To thy fond Lord, and bid him curse himself, That would not hear me ; bid him live on Rooots And Water, and know himself ; he had better Have shunn'd Mankind, than be deserted by them.

[*Ex. Omnes.*

Enter Melissa *and* Chloe.

Mel Who could have thought *Timon* so lost i' th' World ? With what Amazement will the News of this So sudden Alteration be receiv'd by all *Athenians !*

Chl Is it for certain true?

Mel Certain as Death or Fate ! My Father has assur'd me of it, that he is a Bankrupt, his Credit gone, and all His Creditors, with open Jaws, will swallow him 'Tis well I am inform'd, I'll stand upon my Guard.

Enter Page

Page. Madam, a Gentleman below desires Admittance.

Mel See, *Chloe* ; if it be Lord *Timon,* or any one from him, say I am not well. I will not be seen ; be sure I be not.

Chl I warrant you !

Exit Chloe.
Mel.

Mel. Seen by a Bankrupt! no; base Poverty shall
never enter here Oh! were my *Alcibiades* recall'd! he
would adore me still, and wou'd be rich too

Enter Alcibiades *in Difguife, and* Chloe

Chl It is a Gentleman in Difguife, I know him not

Alcibid But my *Meliffa* does   [*Pulls off his Difguife.*

Mel My *Alciciades*! my Hero!
The Gods have hearken'd to my Vows for thee,
And have crown'd all my Wishes Thou'rt more welcome
To me, than the Return of the Sun's Heat
Is to the frozen Region of the North,
That's covered half the Year with Snow and Darknefs.

Alcib My Joy, my Life, my Blood, my Soul, my
And all that's precious in the Earth, I have   [Liberty,
Within my Arms This Treafure far out weighs
The Joys of Conqueft, or Deliverance
From Banifhment and Slavery.

Mel How proud am I of all thy Victories!
'Twas thou that conquer'd, but I triumph'd for thee ;
All Day I figh'd, and wifh'd, and pray'd for thee,
And in the Night thou entertain'dft my Sleeps ;
And whenfoe'er I dreamt thou wert in Danger,
I cry'd out, my *Alcibiades* ! and in my Dreams
Was valiant, and methought I fought for thee

Alcib Oh my divine *Meliffa* ! the Cordial of thy Love
Is of fo ftrong a Spirit, 'twill o'ercome me,
One Kifs, and take my Soul ; another and
'Twill fally out : Oh! I could fix whole Ages on
Thy tender Lip, and pity all the Fools
That keep a fenfelefs Pother in the World for Pow'r,
And Pomp and Noife, and lofe fubftantial Blifs

Mel. There is no Blifs but Love , and but for that
The World would fall in Pieces Oh, with what a Grief
Have I fuftain'd thy Abfence! Had not my Father
Prevented my Efcape, I had come to thee.

Alcib 'Twas well for *Athens* Safety that thou didft not;
I had neglected all my Conquefts which
Preferv'd this bafe, ungrateful Town ; for I
In thee fhou'd have all that I fought for, thou   [me
Would'ft have been Life, Liberty, Country, and Eftate to

Mel

Mel I have the End of all my Hopes and Wishes,
If the ungrateful Senate will let me keep thee

Alcib 'Twas I that made them what they are, in Hopes
They soon would call me home to thee
It was the Thought of that which fir'd my Soul,
At every Stroke the Memory of *Melissa*
Gave Vigour to my Arm, and made me conquer.

Mel. Oh! let Ambition never more disturb
Thy noble Mind! Let Love in Peace possess it
Let not the Noise of Drums and Trumpets Clangor,
Clashing of Arms, and neighing Steeds, and Groans
Of bleeding Men entice thee from me

Alcib The Senate shall not dare remove me from thee.
Should they once offer it, I've an Army will
Toss their usurious Bags about their Ears,
Rifle their Houses, deflour their Wives and Daughters,
And dash their Brains out of their doating Heads.
But dear *Melissa*, since our Hearts so long
Have been united, let's not stay for Friends,
For Ceremony, but come compleat our Joys,
True Love's above senseless Formalities

Mel If any Thing from you could anger me,
This would; but know, none shall invade my Virtue
Without my Life, But on my Knees I vow,
No other Man, tho' crown'd the Emperor
Of all the World, should ever have my Love;
And tho' thy Country basely should desert thee,
I will continue firm.

Alcib And here
I swear, that could I conquer all the Universe,
I'd lay the Crowns and Scepters at thy Feet,
For thee to tread on By thy self I swear,
An Oath more sacred far to me, than all
Mock Deities, which knavish Priests invent,
Are to the poor deluded Rabble.

Ch? Madam! Your Father is come in.

Mel Let us retire My Father has not yet
Forgot his Enmity, the breaking of the
Peace with the *Lacedæmonians,* and his Foil
Which he thinks you caus'd in *Sicily,*

He'll

He'll not forgive.

Alcib Had he injur'd me beyond all Sufferance,
I would forgive him for begetting thee.   [*Exeunt.*

Enter Timon *and Servant.*

Tim Is't poffible? deferted thus? what large Profeffions
did all thefe make but Yefterday? Did they all refufe to
lend, fay you?

1 *Serv* The Rumour of your borrowing was foon
Difpers'd, and then at Sight of one of us
They would ftop, ftart, turn fhort, pafs by, or feem
To overlook us, and avoided us,
As if we had been their mortal Enemies,
And who fufpected not, when they were mov'd,
Came off with bafe Excufes   ['em

Tim. Ye Gods! what will become of *Timon?* I'll go to
My felf, they will not have the Face to ufe me fo.

Enter Demetrius

Oh *Demetrius!* what News bring'ft thou from the Senate?

Dem I am return'd no richer than I went.

Tim. Juft Gods! it cannot be.

Dem They anfwer in a joint and corporate Voice,
That now they are at Ebb, want Treafure, cannot
Do what they would, are forry; you are honourable;
But yet they would have wifh'd; they know not,
Something has been amifs; a noble Nature
May catch a Wrench, would all were well; 'tis Pity;
And fo intending other ferious Matters,
After diftafteful Looks, and thefe hard Fractions,
With certain half Caps, and cold carelefs Nods,
They froze me into Silence.

Tim The Gods reward their Villainy. Old Men
Have their Ingratitude natural to 'em;
Their Blood is cak'd and cold, it feldom flows,
'Tis Want of kindly Warmth which makes 'em cruel,
And Nature, as it grows again towards Earth,
Is fafhion'd for the Journey, dull and heavy.
Heav'n keep my Wits! Or is't a Bleffing to be mad?
Demetrius, follow me; I'll try 'em all my felf,

Dem. The Senate is affembling again,
You'll find 'em in the Senate-houfe.   (*Exeunt.*

Enter

Enter many Creditors with Bills and Papers.
Re-enter Demetrius.

Dem How now! what makes this Swarm of Rascals
here? each looking big, and with the Visage of Demand.

1 *Cred* We wait for certain Sums of Money due.

Dem If Money were as certain as your Waiting,
Why then proffer'd you not your Bills and Bonds,
When your false Masters eat of my Lord's Meat?
Then they would smile and fawn upon him,
And swallow the Interest down their greedy Throats.

Enter Timon *and Servants.*

Tim If *Melissa* be at home, tell her I'll wait on her
suddenly.

1 *Cred* Now let's put in, my Lord, my Bill.

2 *Cred.* Here's mine.

3 *Cred* And mine.

4 *Cred* My Master's.

Tim Hold, hold, my Wits! Knock me down! Cleave
me to the Waist! What would you have, you Harpies?

1 *Cred* We ask our due

Tim Cut my Heart in Pieces, and divide it.

4 *Cred* My Master's is thirty Talents.

Tim. Tell it out of my Blood

2 *Cred* Five Thousand Crowns is mine.

Tim Five thousand Drops pay that.
What's yours, and yours?

3 *Cred.* My Lord.

1 *Cred* My Lord.

Tim Here, take me, pull me in Pieces, will you?
The Gods consume, confound, and rot you all.

1 *Cred* What a Devil, is he mad?

2 *Cred* Mercy on us! let us be gone.

3 *Cred* Let's go, he'll murder some of us

Tim. They've e'en taken my Breath from me. Slaves!
Creditors! Dogs! Preserve my Wits, you Gods!

Dem My Lord, be patient; Passion mends it not.

Lampridius *crosses the Stage, and shuns* Timon

Tim See *Lampridius,* whom I redeem'd out of Prison.
His Father dead since, and he rich. Now the Villain
shuns me.

Enter

Enter Phæax.

Oh ! my good Friend, *Phæax !*

Phæax Oh my Lord !—I'm glad to fee your Lordſhip.
I have a ſudden Occaſion calls me hence,
I'll wait on you inſtantly.   [*Ex.* Phæax.

    Tim. I could not have believ'd this.

Enter Cleon.

My Lord !

    Cleon. Oh my good Lord ! I am going to fee
If I can ſerve your Lordſhip in the Command
I receiv'd from you by your Servant,   [*Ex.* Cleon.

    Tim. O black Ingratitude ! that Villain has
A Jewel at this Moment on, which I preſented him,
Coſt me Three Thouſand Crowns.

    Dem. You'll find 'em all like theſe.

    Tim There are not many ſure ſo bad.
How have I lov'd theſe Men, and ſhewn 'em Kindneſs,
As if they had been my Brothers or my Sons !

Enter Diphilus, *ſeeing* Timon, *muffles his Face, and turns
away.*

Look, is not that my Servant *Diphilas,* whom I marry'd to
The old Man's Daughter, and gave him an Eſtate too ;
And now he hides himſelf, and ſteals from me ?
How much is a Dog more generous than a Man ?
Oblige him once, he'll keep you Company,
Ev'n in your utmoſt Want and Miſery.

Enter Ælius.

Who's that ? *Ælius?* my Lord——*Ælius,*
Demetrius, go let him know *Timon* would ſpeak
With him——   [Dem. *goes to him, he turns back.*
Do you not know me, *Ælius?*

    Ælius. Not know my good Lord *Timon !*

    Tim Think you I have the Plague ?

    Ælius No, my Lord.

    Tim. Why do you ſhun me then ?

    Ælius I ſhun you ! I'd ſerve your Lordſhip with my
      Life.

    Tim I'll not believe, he who would refuſe me Money,
wou'd venture his Life for me.

                              Ælius.

Ælius I am very unfortunate not to have it in my Power to supply you, but I am going to the *Forum* to a Debtor: if I receive any, your Lordship shall command it   [*Ex Ælius*

Tim Had I so lately all the Caps and Knees of the *Athenians,* and is't come to this? Brains hold a little.

Enter Thrasillus

Thras Who's there? *Timon!*   [*Runs back.*

Tim. There's another Villain.

Enter Isander.

How is't *Isander?*

Isand Oh! Heaven! *Timon!*

Tim. What, did I fright you? Am I become so dreadful an Object? Is Poverty contagious?

Isand. Your Lordship ever shall be dear to me. It makes me weep to think I could not serve you, When you sent your Servant. I am expected at the Senate

I humbly ask your Pardon, I'll sell all I have, But I'll supply you soon.   [*Ex.* Isand.

Tim Smooth Tongue, dissembling, weeping Knave, farewel: And farewel all mankind! It shall be so——— *Demetrius?* Go to all these Fellows. Tell 'em I'm supply'd, I have no need of 'em. Set out my Condition to be as good as formerly it has been. That this was but a Tryal: And invite 'em all to Dinner.

Dem My Lord, there's nothing for 'em.

Tim I have taken Order about that.

Dem. What can this mean?   [*Ex.* Demetrius.

Tim I have one Reserve can never fail me, And while *Melissa*'s kind, I can't be miserable; She has a vast Fortune in her own Disposal. The Sun will sooner leave his Course than she Desert me.

Enter first Servant.

Is *Melissa* at Home?

1 *Serv.* She is, my Lord, but will not see you

Tim. What does the Rascal say? Damn'd Villain! To bely her so?   [*Strikes him.*

1 *Serv.*

1 *Serv* By Heav'n 'tis Truth. She says she will not
see you. Her Woman told me so first. And when I
would not believe her, she came and told me so herself:
That she had no Business with you, desired you would not
trouble her, she had Affairs of Consequence, &c.

Tim Now, *Timon*, thou art fallen indeed! Fallen from
all thy Hopes of Happiness Earth open, and swallow
the most miserable Wretch that thou didst ever bear.

Enter Melissa

1 *Serv.* My Lord, *Melissa*'s passing by!

Tim Oh dear *Melissa*!

Mel Is he here? What Luck is this?

Tim. Will you not look on me? not see your *Timon*?
And did not you send me Word so?

Enter Evandra.

Mel I was very busy, and am so now, I must obey my
Father; I am going to him.

Tim. Was it not *Melissa* said, If *Timon* were
Reduc'd to Rags and Misery, and she
Were Queen of all the Universe, she would
Not change her Love?

Mel We can't command our Wills,
Our Fate must be obey'd. [*Ex* Mel.

Tim Some Mountain cover me! and let my Name,
My odious Name be never heard of more!
O straggling Senses, whither are you going!
Farewel, and may we never meet again.
Evandra! How does the Sight of her perplex me!
I've been ungrateful to her, why should I
Blame Villains who are so to me?

Evan *Timon!* I've heard, and felt all thy Afflictions,
I thought I never should have seen thee more;
Nor ever would, hadst thou continu'd prosperous.
Let false *Melissa* basely fly from thee,
Evandra is not made of that coarse Stuff

Tim, Oh turn thy Eyes from an ungrateful Man!

Evan No, since I first beheld my ador'd *Timon*,
They've been fix'd upon thee present, and when absent,
I have each Moment view'd thee in my Mind,
And shall they now remove?

2 *Tim,*

Tim Will thou not fly a wretched Caitiff, who
Has such a Load of Misery beyond
The Strength of human Nature to support ?

Evan I am no base *Athenian* Parasite,
To flye from thy Calamities; I'll help to bear 'em.

Tim Oh! my *Evandra*, they're not to be born
Accursed *Athens!* Forest of two-legg'd Beasts;
Plague, Civil War, and Famine, be thy Lot
Let Propagation cease, that none of thy
Confounding, spurious Brood may ever spring
To infect and damn succeeding Generations:
May every Infant, like the Viper, gnaw
A Passage through his Mother's cursed Womb,
And kill the Hag, or if they fail of it,
May then the Mothers, like fell rav'nous Bitches,
Devour their own base Whelps

Evan *Timon!* compose thy Thoughts; I know thy
And that thy Creditors, like wild Beasts, wait   [Wants,
To prey upon thee, and base *Athens* has,
To its eternal Infamy, deserted thee;
But thy unweary'd Bounty to *Evandra*
Has so enrich'd her, she in Wealth can vie
With any of th'extorting Senators,
And comes to lay it all before thy Feet

Tim Thy most amazing Generosity o'erwhelms me;]
It covers me all o'er with Shame and Blushes.
Thou hast oblig'd a Wretch too much already,
And I have us'd thee ill for't; fly, fly, *Evandra!*
I've Rage and Madness, and I shall infect thee.
Earth! take me to thy Center; open quickly!
Oh that the World were all on Fire!

Evan Oh my dear Lord! this Sight will break my
Take Comfort to you, let your Creditors   (Heart;
Swallow their Maws full; we have yet enough,
Let us retire together, and live free
From all the Smiles and Frowns of human Kind;
I shall have all I wish for, having thee

Tim My Senses are not found, I never can
Deserve thee: I've us'd thee scurvily.

Evan.

Evan. No, my dear *Timon,* thou haſt not:
Comfort thy ſelf; if thou haſt been unkind,
Forgive thy ſelf, and I forgive thee for it.

Tim I never will;
Nor will I be oblig'd to one
I've treated ſo injuriouſly as her——   [*Aſide.*

Evan Pray, my Lord, go home; ſtrive to compoſe
Your ſelf All that I have was and is yours, I wiſh
It ne'er had been, that I might have ſhewn,
By ſtronger Proofs, how much I love my *Timon.*

Tim. Moſt Excellent of all the whole Creation!
Thou art too good that thou ſhould'ſt e'er partake
Of my Misfortunes——
And I'm reſolv'd not to involve her in 'em.   [*Aſide.*
Prithee, *Evandra,* go to thy own Houſe,
I am once more to give my flattering Rogues
An Entertainment' but ſuch a one as ſhall befit'em'
And then I'll ſee thee

Evan Heav'n ever bleſs my Dear. [*Ex.* Tim. *and* Ev.
Enter Phæax, Cleon, Iſander, Iſidore, Thraſillus, Ælius.

Phæax. I think my honourable Lord did but try us.

Cleon On my Life it was no more. His Steward aſ-
ſur'd me, his Condition was near as good as ever.

Iſand That I doubt——but 'tis well at preſent, by his
new feaſting

Ælius. I am ſorry I was not furniſh'd when he ſent to
me

Iſid. I am ſick of that Grief, now I ſee how all things go.
            Enter Timon *and Attendants*

Tim. Oh' my kind Friends' How is't with you all ?
How I rejoice to ſee you'——Come, ſerve in Dinner.

Phæax My noble Lord' never ſo well as when your
Lordſhip is ſo

Ælius I am ſick with Shame, that I ſhould be ſo unfortunate a Beggar when you ſent to me.

Tim. No more, no more, I did but make Trial' I
have no Need of any Sums, my Eſtate is in good Health
ſtill

Phæax Trial' my good Lord Would any one refuſe
9   B b   your

your Lordſhip, were it in his Power? Command half my
Eſtate! I'm ſorry I was ſo in haſte, I could not ſtay to tell
you this I have receiv'd Bills, even now Pray uſe me
—I hope he will not take me at my Word   [*Aſide.*

Iſand Take it not unkindly, my good Lord, that I
could not ſerve you. Now, my Lord, command me——
I am able

Tim I beſeech you do not think on't: I know ye love
me, all of ye

Phæax Equal with our ſelves, my dear Lord.

Thraſ If you had ſent but two Hours before to me—

Cleon Now I have Money, pray command it.

Tim. No more, for Heaven's Sake ! think you I diſtruſt
My kind good Friends ! you are the beſt of Friends.
My Fortune ne'er ſhall drive me from you, and ſhould
Mine fail, which I hope it never will,
I know I may command all yours.

Phæax. I ſhall think my ſelf happy enough, if you
would but command my utmoſt Drachma.

Ælius. That were Honour indeed to ſerve Lord *Timon,*
I would with Life and Fortune

Iſand Alas ! who would not be proud of it?

Iſid. Not a Man in *Athens.*

Cleon There's no Foot of my Eſtate your Lordſhip may
not call your own

Thraſ Nor mine, my noble Lord !

Tim Thanks to my worthy Friends.
Who has ſuch kind, ſuch hearty Friends as I have ?

Ælius. All cover'd Diſhes

Iſand Royal Chear, I warrant you.

Phæax Doubt not of that, if Money or the Seaſon can
afford it.

Iſid The ſame good Lord ſtill.

Tim Come, my worthy Friends, let's ſit: Make it
not a City Feaſt, to let the Meat cool ere we agree upon
our Places.

The GRACE.

YOU *great Benefactors, make your felves prais'd for your own Gifts, bafe, ungrateful Man will not do it of himfelf, referve ftill to give, left your Deities be defpis'd, were your Godheads to borrow of Men, Men would forfake ye Make the Meat belov'd more than the Man that gives it Let no Affembly of twenty be without a Score of Villains If there be twelve Women, let a Dozen of 'em be ———— as they are Confound, I befeech you, all the Senators of Athens, together with the common People What is amifs make fit for Deftruction, for thefe my prefent Friends, as they are to me nothing, fo in nothing blefs them, and to nothing are they welcome, but Toads and Snakes. A Feaft fit for fuch venemous Knaves.*

Phæax What does he mean ?
Ælius. He's mad, I think
Tim May you a better Feaft never behold.
You Knot of Mouth-Friends, Vapours, luke-warm Knaves;
Moft fmiling, fmooth, detefted Parafites ;
Courteous Deftroyers, affable Wolves, meek Bears ;
You Fools of Fortune, Trencher-Friends, Time-Flies,
Cap and Knee-Slaves ; an everlafting Leprofie
Cruft you quite o'er !——What, do'ft thou fteal away ?
Soft, take thy Phyfick firft , and thou, and thou ;
Stay, I will lend thee Money——borrow none.
Phæax What means your Lordfhip? I'll be gone.
Cleon And I. He'll murder us
Ælius. This is raging Madnefs, fly, fly
[*They run off*

Tim. What all in Motion! henceforth be no Feaft,
Whereat a Villain's not a welcome Gueft
Burn Houfe, fink Athens ; henceforth hated be,
Of Timon, Man, and all Humanity. [Ex. *Tim.*

ACT IV. SCENE I.

Timon *Solus.*

Tim LET me look back upon thee! Oh thou Wall
That gird'eft in thofe Wolves! Sink in theEarth,
And fence not *Athens* longer, that vile Den
Of favage Beafts, ye Matrons all turn Whores,
Obedience fail in Children; Slaves and Fools
Pluck the grave wrinkled Senate from the Bench,
And minifter in their ftead. To general Filths
Convert o'th' inftant green Virginity,
Do't in their Parents Eyes. Bankrupts, hold faft,
Rather than render back; out with your Knives,
And cut your Trufters Throat Bound Servants, fteal;
Large-handed Robbers your grave Mafters are,
And pill by Law. Maid, to thy Mafter's Bed;
Miftrefs, to the Brothel Son of twenty-one,
Pluck the lin'd Crutch from thy old limping Sire:
And with it beat his Brains out Piety, Fear,
Religion to the Gods, Peace, Juftice, Truth,
Domeftick Awe, Night-Reft, and Neighbourhood,
Inftruction, Manners, Myfteries and Trades,
Degrees, Obfervations, Cuftoms and Laws,
Decline to your confounding Contraries,
And let Confufion live Plagues incident to Men,
Your potent and infectious Feavers heap
On *Athens,* ripe for Vengeance Cold *Sciatica,*
Cripple the Senators, that their Limbs may halt
As lamely as their Manners. Luft and Liberty,
Creep in the Minds and Marrows of your Youth,
That 'gainft the Stream of Virtue they may ftrive,
And drown themfelves in Riot. Itches, Blains,

Sow all the *Athenians* Bosoms, and their Crop
Be general Leprosie.   Breath infect Breath,
That their Society, as their Friendship, may
Be merely Poison.   Nothing, nothing I bear from thee:
Farewel, thou most detested Town! and sudden
Ruin swallow thee.   [*Ex.* Timon.

SCENE *the Senate-House, all the Senate sitting.*

Enter Alcibiades.

Nic. How dare you, *Alcibiades,*
Knowing your Sentence not recall'd, venture hither?
    Alcib You see, my rev'rend Lords, what Confidence
I place in you, that durst expose my Person
Before my Sentence be recall'd. I am not now
Petitioner for my self; I leave my Case
To your good and generous Natures, when you shall
Think I've deserv'd your Favour for my Service.
I am an humble Suitor to your Vertue,
(For Mercy is the Vertue of the Law,
And none but Tyrants use it cruelly)
'Tis for a gallant Officer of mine,
As brave a Man as e'er drew Sword for *Athens*;
'Tis *Thrasibulus,* who, in heat of Blood,
Has stept into the Law above his Depth.
    Nic. True, he has kill'd a Man.
    Alcib I've been before
Before the *Areopagus,* and they refuse
All Mercy.   He is a Man
(Setting his Fate aside) of comely Vertues;
Nor did he soil the Fact with Cowardise,
But with a noble Fury did revenge
His injur'd Reputation
    Phæax. You strive to make an ugly Deed look fair.
    Nic As if you'd bring Manslaug'ter into Form,
And Valour did consist in quarrelling
    Æluz That is a base and illegitimate Valour.
He's truly valiant that can wisely suffer
    Isand. All single Combats are detestable;
                        B b 3   And

And Courage that's not warranted by Law
Is much too dangerous a Vice to go unpunish'd.
Isd If Injuries be evil, Death is most ill .
And then what Folly is't, for the less Ill
To hazard Life, the chiefest Good ?
   Cleon There's no such Courage as in bearing Wrong.
   Alcib If there be such Valour in bearing, what
Do we abroad ? Women are then more valiant,
That stay at home , and the Ass a better Captain
Than is the Lion   The Malefactor, that is
Loaden with Irons, wiser than the Judge
   Nic You cannot make gross Sins look clean
With Eloquence
   Alcib Why do fond Men expose themselves to Battel,
And not endure all Threats, and sleep upon 'em,
And let the Foes quietly cut their Throats ?
Come, my Lords — be pitiful and good
   Nic He that's more merciful than Law, is cruel.
   Alcib The utmost Law is downright Tyranny .
To kill, I grant, is the extreamest Guilt,
But in Defence of Honour ————
   Pleon Honour ! is any Honour to be sought for
But the Honour of our Country ?
   Alcib Who will not fight for's own, will never fight
For that   Let him that has no Anger judge him :
How many in their Anger would commit
This Captain's Fau't — had they but Courage for't ?
   Cleon You speak in vain
   Alcib If you will not excuse his Crime, consider
Who he is, and what he has done !
His Service at *Lacedæmon* and *Byzantium*
Are Bribes sufficient for his Life
   Nic. He did his Duty, and was rewarded with
his Pay , and if he did not do it, he should be pu-
nish'd
   Alcib How, my Lords ! is that all the Return
For Soldiers Toi's, fasting and watching ,
The many cruel Hardships which they suffer ,
The Multitude of Hazards, Blood, and Loss
Of Limbs ?

                           Isand.

Isand Come, you urge it too far; he dies.

Alcib. He has flain in Fight Hundreds of Enemies.
How full of Valour did he bear himfelf
In the laft Conflict! What Death and Wounds he gave!

Isid H' has given too many

Ælius. He is a known Rioter, he has a Sin
That often drowns him; in that beaftly Fury
He has committed Outrages

Phæax Such as we fhall not name, fince others were
Concern'd in 'em, you know.

Nic. In fhort,
His Days are foul, and Nights are dangerous;
And he muft die.

Alcib. Hard Fate! he might have dy'd nobly in Fight,
And done you Service. If not for his Deferts,
Confider all my Actions, Lords, and join 'em
With his—your reverend Ages love Security,
And therefore fhou'd cherifh thofe that give it you.

Phæax You are too bold—he dies—No more——

Alcib. Too bold, Lord! Do you know who I am?

Cleon. What fays he?

Alcib. Call me to your Remembrances.

Isand Confider well the Place, and who we are!

Alcib I cannot think but you have forgotten me.
Muft I fue for fuch common Grace,
And be deny'd? my Wounds ake at you!

Nic Y'are infolent! we have not forgotten yet
Your Riot and deftructive Vices; Whoredoms,
Profanenefs, giddy-headed Paffions.

Phæax. Your breaking *Mercury*'s Statues, and mocking
The Myfteries of facred *Proferpine.*

Alcib. Infolent! now you provoke me; I'm vext to fee
Your private Malice vented in a Place
Where honeft Men would only think
On publick Intereft. 'Tis bafe, and in another Place
You would not fpeak thus.

Nic. How fay you!

Alcib I thought the Images of *Mercury,*
And the Rites of *Proferpine,*
Had only been the Favourites o' th' Rabble:

5   Thefe

These things are Mockery to Men of Sense.
What Folly 'tis to worship Statues, when
You'd kick the Rogues that made 'em!
　　Phæax. How dare you talk thus? you have been a Rebel.
　　Alcib. Could any but the basest of Mankind
Urge that to me, by whom he keeps that Head
That utters this against me? my Rebellion!
It was 'gainst the common People; and you all
Are Rebels against them
　　Nic. Cease your Insolence! we sided not with *Spartans.*
　　Alcib. What Means had I to humble th' *Athenian*
Rabble, but that?
　　Phæax. It was well done, to get your Friend King *Agis*
his Wife with Child, in his Absence.
　　Alcib. He was a Blockhead, and I mended his Breed for
　　him————
But what is that to the Matter now in hand?
You have provok'd me, Lords, and I must tell you,
It is by me you sit in Safety here.
　　Phæax By you! bold Man!
　　Alcib Yes, by me! fearful Man!
You have incens'd me now beyond all Patience;
And I must tell you what ye owe me, Lords.
'Twas I that kept great *Tissaphernes* from
The *Spartans* Aid, by which *Athens*, by this,
Had been one Heap of Rubbish; I stopt
A Hundred and Fifty Gallies from *Phœnicia,*
Which would have fallen upon you· 'Twas I made
This *Tissaphernes Athens*' Friend, upon Condition
That they would awe the common People, and take
The Government into the best Mens Hands.
Would you were so! I sent *Pisander* then
To form this *Aristocracy,* and promis'd
The *Persian* Generals Forces to assist you;
And when you had this Pow'r, ye cast me off
That got it you
　　Nic. My Lords, led him be silenc'd,
Shall he thus beard the Senate?
　　Alcib I will be heard, and then your Pleasure, Lords.
Did not your Army, in the Isle of *Samos,*
Offended

Offended at your Government, chufe me General,
And would have march'd to your Deftruction ?
Which I diverted In that Time your Foes
Would foon have won the Country of *Ionia*,
Of th' *Hellefpont*, and all the other Ifles,
While you had been employ'd at home
With Civil Wars I kept fome back by Force,
And by fair Words others ; in which, *Thrafibulus*,
This Man of *Stiria*, whom you thus condemn,
Having the loudeft Voice of all the *Athenians*,
Employ'd by me, cry'd out to all the Army ;
And thus we kept 'em from you, Lords, and now
Athens a fecond Time was fav'd by me.

   Phæax. 'Tis a Shame that we fhould fuffer this !
   Alcib 'Tis a Shame thefe Things are unrewarded.
Another Time I kept Five Hundred Sail
Of the *Phænicians* from the Aid
Of the *Lacedæmonians*, won from 'em a Sea-Battle,
Before the City of *Abidus*,
In Spight of *Pharnabazus*' mighty Power.
Think on my Victory at *Cizicum*, where I
Slew *Mendorus* in the Field, and took the City ;
I brought then the *Bithynians* to your Yoke,
Won *Silibræa* on the *Hellefpont* ;
And then *Byzantium*. Thus not only I
Diverted the Torrent of the Army's Fury
From you, but turn'd it on the Enemies ;
And all the While you fafely told your Money,
And let it out upon extorted Intereft :
Muft I be after all poorly deny'd
His Life who has fo often ventur'd it for you ?

   Phæax He dies, and you deferve it, but our Sentence
Is, for your Infolence, we banifh you ·
If you be two Hours more within thefe Walls,
Your Head is forfeited. Do you all confent ?

   All Sen All, All !
   Alcib All ! All ! I am glad I know you all !
Banifh me ! Banifh your Dotage ! your Extortion !
Banifh your foul Corruptions and Self-Ends !
Oh the bafe Spirit of a Common-wealth !

One

One Tyrant is much better than Four Hundred .
The worst of Kings would be asham'd of this.
I am only rich in my large Hurts for you ;
Is this the Balsam the ill-natur'd Senate
Pours into Captains Wounds ? ha ! Banishment?
A good Man would not stay with you , I embrace
My Sentence . 'Tis a Cause that's worthy of me.

           [*Exit Alcib.*

 Nic. Was ever——heard such daring Insolence ?
Shall we break up the Senate ?

  All Sen Ay, ay.   [*Exeunt.*

    Timon *in the Woods digging*
 Tim O blessed breeding Sun ! draw from the Fens,
The Bogs, and muddy Marshes, and from
Corrupted standing Lakes, rotten Humidity,
Enough to infect the Air with dire consuming Pestilence,
And let the poisonous Exhalations fall
Down on th' *Athenians* , they are all Flatterers,
And so is all Mankind
For every Degree of Fortune's smooth'd
And sooth'd by that below it ; the learned Pate
Ducks to the Golden Fool , there's nothing level
In our Conditions, but base Villainy ;
Therefore be abhorr'd, each Man, and all Society ;
Earth, yield me Roots; thou common Whore of Man-
  kind,
That put'st such Odds amongst the Rout of Nations,
I'll make thee do thy right Office Ha ! what's here ?
Gold ! yellow, glittering, precious Gold! enough
To purchase my Estate again Let me see further .
What a vast Mass of Treasure's here ! There lie;
I will use none ; 'twill bring me Flatterers.
I'll send a Pattern on't to the *Athenians,*
And let 'em know what a vast Mass I've found,
Which I'll keep from 'em I think I see a Passenger
Not far off, I'll send it by him to the Senate [*Ex.* Tim.

    Enter Evandra
 Evan How long shall I seek my unhappy Lord ?
But I will find him, or will lose my Life
Oh ! base and shameful Villainy of Man ;

          Amongst

Amongſt ſo many Thouſands he has oblig'd,
Not one would follow him in his Afflictions!
Ha! here is a Spade! ſure this belongs to ſome one
Who's not far off; I will enquire of him.

Enter Timon.

Tim. Who's there? What Beaſt art thou that com'ſt
To trouble me?

Evan. Pray do not hurt me; I am come to ſeek
The poor diſtreſſed *Timon*; did you ſee him?

Tim. If thou be'ſt born of wicked human Race,
Why com'ſt thou hither to diſturb his Mind?
He has forſworn all Company.

Evan. Is this my Lord? oh dreadful Transformation!
My deareſt Lord, do you not know me?

Tim. Thou walk'ſt upon two Legs, and haſt a Face
Erect t'wards Heav'n; and all ſuch Animals
I have abjur'd, they are not honeſt;
Thoſe Creatures that are ſo, walk on all four.
Prithee, be gone.

Evan. He's much diſtracted ſure! Have you forgotten
Your poor *Evandra?*

Tim. No; I remember there was ſuch a one,
Whom I us'd ill! Why do'ſt thou follow Miſery,
And add to it? Prithee be gone

Evan. Theſe cruel Words will break my Heart, I
          come
Not to increaſe thy Miſery, but mend it
Ah! my dear *Timon*, why this Slave-like Habit!
And why this Spade?

Tim. 'Tis to dig Roots, and earn my Dinner with.

Evan. I have converted Part of my Eſtate
To Money and to Jewels, and have brought 'em
To lay 'em at thy Feet, and the Remainder
Thou ſoon ſhalt have.

Tim. I will not touch 'em; no, I ſhall be flatter'd.

Evan. Comfort thy ſelf, and quit this ſavage Life;
We have enough, in Spite of all the Baſeneſs
Of th' *Athenians*: Let not thoſe Slaves
Triumph o'er thy Afflictions; we'll live free.

                                        Tim.

Tim. If thou diffwad'ft me from this Life, thou hat'ft
For all the Principalities on Earth   [me.
I would not change this Spade! prithee begone,
Thou temp'ft me but in vain

   Evan Be not fo cruel.
Nothing but Death fhall ever take me from thee.

   Tim I'll never change my Life · What would'ft thou do
With me ?

   Evan, I'd live the fame   Is there a Time or Place,
A Temper or Condition I would leave
My *Timon* in ?

   Tim You muft not ftay with me.

   Evan Oh too unkind!
I offered thee all my Profperity———
And thou moft niggardly denieft me Part
Of thy Afflictions

   Tim Ah foft *Evandra!* is not the bleak Air
Too boifterous a Chamberlain for thee ?
Or do'ft thou think thefe reverend Trees that have
Out-liv'd the Raven, will be Pages to thee ?
And fkip where thou appoint'ft 'em ? Will the Brook
Candid with Morning Ice, be Caudle to thee ?

   Evan Thou wilt be all to me

   Tim I'm favage as a Satyr, and my Temper
Is much unfound, my Brain will be diftracted.

   Evan Thou wilt be *Timon* ftill, that's all I afk.

   Tim It was a Comfort to me, when I thought
That thou wer't profperous, thou art too good
To fuffer with me the rough boift'rous Weather,
To mortify thy felf with Roots and Water,
'Twill kill thee   Prithee begone

   Evan To Death, if you command

   Tim I have forefworn all human Converfation.

   Evan And fo have I but thine

   Tim 'Twill then be Mifery indeed to fee
Thee bear it

   Evan On my Knees I beg it.
If thou refufeft me, I'll kill my felf,
I fwear by all the Gods

   Tim Rife, my *Evandra* !

I

I now pronounce to all the World, there is
One Woman honeft; if they afk me more,
I will not grant it . Come, my dear *Evandra*,
I'll fhew thee Wealth enough I found with Digging,
To purchafe all my Land again, which I
Will hide from all Mankind.

 Evan. Put all my Gold and Jewels to't:

 Tim. Well faid, *Evandra !* Look, here is enough
To make black white, foul fair, wrong right,
Bafe noble, old young, Cowards valiant,
Ye Gods! here is enough to lug your Priefts
And Servants from your Altars. This Thing can
Make the hoar'd Leprofy ador'd, place Thieves,
And give 'em Title, Knee and Approbation ;
This makes the toothlefs, warp'd, and wither'd Widow
Marry again. This can embalm and fweeten
Such as the Spittle houfe and ulcerous Creatures
Would caft the Gorge at : This can defile
The pureft Bed, and make Divorce 'twixt Son
And Father, Friends and Kindred; all Society ;
Can bring up new Religions, and kill Kings.

 Evan. Let th' Earth that breeds it, Hide it, there 'twill
  fleep,
And do no hired Mifchief

 Tim. Now Earth for a Root

 Evan 'Tis her unfathom'd Womb teems and feeds all ;
And of fuch vile corrupting Metal, as
Man, her proud arrogant Child is made of, does
Engender black Toads, and Adders blue, the gilded Newt
And Eye lefs venom'd Worm, with all
The loathfome Births the quickning Sun does fhine on

 Tim. Yield him, who all thy human Sons does hate,
From out thy plenteous Bofom fome poor Roots ;
Sear up thy fertile Womb to all Things elfe ,
Dry up thy Marrow, thy Veins, thy Tilth and Pafture,
Whereof ungrateful Man with liquorifh Draughts
And unctuous Morfels, greafes his pure Mind,
That from it all Confideration flips
But hold a While——I am faint and weary,
My tender Hands, not us'd to toil, are gall'd.

    C c   *Evan*

Evan. Repofe your felf, my deareft Love thus—your
       Head
Upon my Lap, and when thou haft refrefh'd
Thy felf, I'll gather Fruits and Berries for thee.

Enter Apemantus.

Tim More Plague ! More Man ! retire into my Cave.
                                        [*Exit* Evan.

Apem. I was directed hither ;—Men report,
That thou affect'ft my Manners, and do'ft ufe 'em.

Tim 'Tis then becaufe I would not keep a Dog
Should imitate thee.

Apem. This is in thee a Nature but infected,
A poor unmanly Melancholy, fprung
From Change of Fortune.   Why this Spade ? this Place ?
This Slave-like Habit, and thefe Looks of Care ?
Thy fordid Flatt'rers yet wear Silk, lye foft,
Hug their difeas'd Perfumes, and have forgotten
That ever *Timon* was.   Shame not thefe Woods,
By putting on the Cunning of a Carpet.
Be thou a Flatt'rer now, and feek to thrive
By that which has undone thee.   Hinge thy Knee,
And let each Great Man's Breath blow off thy Cap,
Praife his moft monftrous Deformities,
And call his fouleft Vices excellent.
Thou wer't us'd thus.

Tim Do'ft thou love to hear thy felf prate ?

Apem No, but thou fhould'ft hear me fpeak.

Tim I hate thy Speech, and fpit at thee.

Apem. Do not affume my Likenefs to difgrace it.

Tim Were I like thee, I'd ufe the Copy,
As the Original fhould be us'd.

Apem How fhould it be us'd ?

Tim. It fhould be hang'd.

Apem. Before thou wer't a Madman, now a Fool;
Art thou proud ftill ? Call any of thofe Creatures,
Whofe naked Natures live in all the Spite
Of angry Heav'n, whofe bare unhoufed Trunks
To the conflicting Elements expos'd,
Anfwer mere Nature, bid 'em flatter thee,
And thou fhalt find———

                                        Tim.

Tim. An Aſs of thee.——

Apem. I love thee better now than e'er I did——

Tim. I hate thee worſe——

Apem. Why ſo ?

Tim Thou flattereſt Miſery.

Apem. I flatter not, but ſay thou art a Wretch——

Tim. Why do'ſt thou ſeek me out ?

Apem Perhaps to vex thee.

Tim. Always a Villain's Office, or a Fool's.

Apem If thou did'ſt put on this ſoure Life and Habit,
To caſtigate thy Pride, 'twere well; but thou
Do'ſt it inforc'dly, wer't thou not a Beggar,
Thou'd'ſt be a Courtier again.

Tim Slave, thou ly'ſt; 'tis next thee the laſt Thing
Which I would be on Earth.

Apem. How much does willing Poverty excel
Uncertain Pomp! for this is filling ſtill,
Never compleat, that alway at high Wiſh;
But thou haſt a contentleſs, wretched Being;
Thou ſhou'dſt deſire to die, being miſerable.

Tim Not by his Advice that is more miſerable.

Apem. I am contented with my Poverty.

Tim. Thou ly'ſt; thou would'ſt not ſnarl ſo if thou
But 'tis a Burthen that is light to thee,   [wer't
For thou haſt been always us'd to carry it.
Thou art a Thing whom Fortune's tender Arms
With Favour never claſp'd, but bred a Dog.
Had'ſt thou, like me, from thy firſt Swath proceeded
To all the ſweet Degrees that this brief World
Afforded me, thou would'ſt have plung'd thy ſelf
In general Riot, melted down thy Youth
In different Beds of Luſt, and never learnt
The icy Precepts of Morality,
But had'ſt purſu'd th' alluring Game before thee

Apem. Thou ly'ſt—I would have liv'd juſt as I do.

Tim Poor Slave! thou do'ſt not know thyſelf! thou well
Can'ſt bear what thou haſt been bred to; but for me,
Who had the World as my Confectionary,
The Tongues, the Eyes, the Ears, the Hearts of all Men,
At Duty more than I could frame Employments for,

C 2   That

That numberlefs upon me ftuck, as Leaves
Upon the Oak, they've with one Winter's Brufh
Fal'n from their Boughs, and let me open, bare
To every Storm that blows, for me to bear this,
Who never knew but better, is a great Burthen:
Thy Nature did commence in Suff'rance   Time
Hath made thee hard in't   Why fhould'ft thou hate Men?
They never flatter'd thee. If thou wilt curfe,
Curfe then thy Father, who in Spight put Stuff
To fome She-Beggar, and compounded thee,
A poor, hereditary Rogue.

    Apem. Poor Afs!
The Middle of Humanity thou ne'er
Did'ft know, but the Extremity of both Ends:
When thou we'rt in thy Guilt and thy Perfumes
Men mock'd thee for thy too much Curiofity;
Thou in thy Rags know'ft none

    Tim Begone, thou tedious prating Fool.
That the whole Life of *Athens* were in this
One Root, thus would I eat it.

    Apem I'll mend thy Feaft.

    Tim Mend my Condition, take thy felf away.

    Apem What would'ft thou have to *Athens*?

    Tim. Thee thither in a Whirlwind

    Apem When I have nothing elfe to do, I'll fee thee again.

    Tim If there were nothing living but thy felf
Thou fhould'ft not even then be welcome to me;
I had rather be a Beggar's Dog than *Apemantus.*

    Apem Thou art a miferable Fool

    Tim Would thou wer't clean enough to fpit upon.

    Apem Thou art too bad to curfe, no Mifery
That I could wifh thee but thou haft already.

    Tim Be gone, thou Iffue of a mangy Dog.
I fwoon to fee thee

    Apem Would thou would'ft burft.

    Tim. Away, thou tedious Rogue, or I'll cleave thy Scull.

    Apem Farewel, Beaft

    Tim Be gone, Toad

    Apem The *Athenians* report thou haft found a Mafs
                    of

of Treafure; they'll find thee out   The Plague of Company light on thee.

Tim. Slave! Dog! Viper! out of my Sight
　　　　　　　　　　　　　　[*Exit* Apemantus.
Choler will kill me if I fee Mankind!
Come forth, *Evandra*; thou art kind and good.
　　　　　　　Enter Evandra.
Can'ft thou eat Roots, and drink at that frefh Spring?
Our Feafting's come to this

Evan. Whate'er I eat
Or drink with thee is Feaft enough to me;
Would'ft thou compofe thy Thoughts, and be content.
I fhou'd be happy.　　-　　　　　　　　[Brook,

Tim Let's quench our Thirft at yonder murmuring
And then repofe a while　　　　　　　[*Exeunt.*
　　　　Enter Poet, Painter, *and* Mufician

Poet. As I took Note o' th' Place, it cannot be far off
where he abides.

Muf Does the Rumour hold for certain, that he's fo
full of Gold?

Poet 'Tis true! H'has found an infinite Store of Gold,
He has fent a Pattern of it to the Senate,
You will fee him a Palm again in *Athens,*
And flourifh with the higheft of 'em all;
Therefore 'tis fit, in this fuppos'd Diftrefs,
We tender all our Services to him——

Paint. If the Report be true, we fhall fucceed.

Muf. If we fhou'd not——
　　　　Re enter Timon *and* Evandra

Poet. We'll venture our joint Labours.   Yon is he,
I know by the Defcription

Muf. Let's hide our felves, and fee how he will take it.
　　　　　　　　　　　　　　[*A Symphony.*

Evan Here's Mufick in the Woods, whence comes it?

Tim. From flattering Rogues, who have heard that I
have Gold, but that their Difappointment would be greater, in taking Pains for nought, I'd fend 'em back——

Poet Hail, worthy *Timon!*——.

Muf. Our moft noble Mafter——

Paint. My moft excellent Lord!

　　　　　　　　C c 3　　　　　　　　　*Tim.*

Tim. Have I once liv'd to fee three honeft Men?

Poet. Having fo often tafted of your Bounty,
And hearing you were retir'd, your Friends fall'n off,
For whofe ungrateful Natures we are griev'd,
We come to do you Service.

Muf. We are not of fo bafe a Mold, we fhould
Defert our noble Patron.

Tim Moft honeft Men! oh! how fhall I requite you?
Can you eat Roots, and drink cold Water?

Poet. Whate'er we can we will, to do you Service.

Tim Good Men! come, you are honeft, you have heard
That I have Gold enough! fpeak Truth, ye're honeft.

Poet. So it is faid; but therefore came we not.

Muf. Not we, my Lord!

Paint. We thought not of it.

Tim You are good Men, but have one mon'ftrous Fault.

Poet. I befeech your Honour what is it?

Tim. Each of you trufts a damn'd notorious Knave.

Paint Who is that, my Lord?

Tim Why, one another, and each trufts himfelf.
Ye bafe Knaves, tripartite! begone? make hafte!
Or I will ufe you fo like Knaves!　　　　［*He ftones 'em.*

Poet. Fy, fly,——　　　　　　　　　　［*All ran out.*

Tim How fick am I of this falfe World? I'll now
Prepare my Grave, to lie where the light Foam
Of the Outrageous Sea may wafh my Corp'.

Evan. My deareft *Timon,* do not talk of Death;
My Life and thine together muft determine.

Tim There is no Reft without it; prithee leave
My wretched Fortune, and live long and happy,
Without thy *Timon;* there is Wealth enough.

Evan. I have no Wealth but thee; let us lie down to reft;
I am very faint and heavy——　　　　［*They lie down.*
　　　　　　Enter Meliffa *and* Chloe.

Mel Let the Chariot ftay there. It is moft certain he
has found a Mafs of Money; and he has fent Word to the
Senate, he is richer than ever.

Chl. Sure, were he rich, he would appear again.

Mel. If he be, I doubt not but with my Love I'll charm
　　　　　　　　　　　　　　　　　　him

him back to *Athens*; 'twas my deferting him has made
him thus melancholly.

Chl. If he be not, you'll promife Love in vain.

Mel. If he be not, my Promife fhall be vain,
For I'll be fure to break it; Thus you faw,
When *Alcibiades* was banifh'd laft,
I would not fee him; I am always true
To Intereft and to myfelf. There Lord *Timon* lies!

Tim. What Wretch art thou, come to difturb me?

Mel. I am one that loves thee fo, I cannot lofe thee;
I am gotten from my Father and my Friends,
To call thee back to *Athens*, and her Arms
Who cannot live without thee.

Evan. It is *Meliffa*; prithee, liften not
To her deftructive *Syren*'s Voice.

Tim. Fear not.

Mel. Do'ft thou not know thy dear *Meliffa*,
To whom thou mad'ft fuch Vows?

Tim. O yes, I know that Piece of Vanity,
That frail, proud, inconftant, foolifh thing.
I do remember once upon a time,
She fwore eternal Love to me; foon after,
She would not fee me, fhunn'd me, flighted me.

Mel. Ah now I fee thou never lov'dft me, *Timon!*
That was a Tryal which I made of thee,
To find if thou did'ft love me; if thou had'ft,
Thou would'ft have borne it: I lov'd thee then much more
Than all the World—but thou art falfe, I fee,
And any little Change can drive thee from me,
And thou wilt leave me miferable.

Evan. Mind not that Crocodile's Tears,
She would betray thee.

Mel. Is there no Truth among Mankind? Had I
So much Ingratitude, I had left
Thy fallen Fortune, and ne'er feen thee more:
Ah *Timon!* could'ft thou have been kind, I could
Rather have begg'd with thee, than have enjoy'd
With any other all the Pomp of *Greece*;
But thou art loft, and haft forgotten all thy Oaths.

Evan. Why fhou'd you ftrive to invade another's Right?
He's

He's mine, for ever mine . Thefe Arms
Shall keep him from thee.   [fo?

Mel. Thine! poor mean Fool! has Marriage made him
No——Thou'rt his Concubine, difhoneft Thing,
I would enjoy him honeftly.

Tim. Peace, Screech-Owl! There is much more Honefty
In this one Woman, than in all thy Sex
Blended together, Our Hearts are one,
And fhe is mine for ever.   Wer't thou the Queen
Of all the Univerfe, I would not change her for thee.

Evan Oh my dear Lord! This is a better Cordial ·
Than all the World can give.

Tim. Falfe! proud! affected! vain fantaftick Thing!
Begone, I would not fee thee, unlefs I were
A Bafilifk . Thou boaft'ft that thou art honeft of thy Body,
As if the Body made one honeft : Thou haft a vile
Corrupted filthy Mind————

Mel I am no Whore as fhe is.

Tim Thou ly'ft, fhe's none. But thou art one in thy Soul.
Begone, or thoul't prove me to do a thing unmanly,
And beat thee hence

Mel Farewel Beaft——   [*Ex.* Mel. *and* Chloe.

Enan Let me kifs thy Hand, my deareft Lord,
If it were poffible, more dear than ever

Tim *Let's now go feek fome Reft within my Cave,*
If any we can have without the Grave.   [Exeunt.

ACT

ACT V. SCENE I.

Enter Timon *and* Evandra.

Tim NOW after all the Follies of this Life,
    Timon has made his everlasting Mansion
Upon the beached Verge of the Salt Flood,
Where every Day the swelling Surge shall wash him:
There he shall rest from all the Villanies,
Betraying Smiles, or th' oppressing Frowns
Of proud and impotent Man

Evan. Speak not of Death, I cannot lose thee yet,
Throw off this dire, consuming Melancholy.
Oh could'st thou love as I do, thou'd'st not have
Another Wish but me. There is no State on Earth
Which I can envy while I've thee within
These Arms——take Comfort to thee, think not yet
Of Death——leave not *Evandra* yet

Tim Think'st thou in Death we shall not think,
And know, and love, better than we can here?
Oh yes, *Evandra!* There our Happiness
Will be without a Wish——I feel my long Sickness
Of Health and Living now begin to mend,
And nothing will bring me all things: Thou, *Evandra,*
Art the thing alone on Earth would make me wish
To play my Part upon the troublesome Stage,
Where Folly, Madness, Falshood, and Cruelty,
Are the only Actions represented

Evan That I have lov'd my *Timon* faithfully,
Without one erring Thought, the Gods can witness;
And as my Life was true, my Death shall be;
If I one Minute after thee survive,
The Scorn and Infamy of all my Sex
Light on me, and may I live to be
Melissa's Slave.

5   *Tim.*

Tim. Oh my ador'd *Evandra!*
Thy Kindness covers me with Shame and Grief,
I have deserv'd so little from thee;
Wer't not for thee I'd wish the World on Fire.

Enter Nicias, Phæax, Isidore, Isander, Cleon, Thrasillus, *and* Ælius.

More Plagues yet!
Nic. How does the worthy *Timon?*
It grieves our Hearts to see thy low Condition,
And we are come to mend it
Phæax. We and th'*Athenians* cannot live without thee;
Cast from thee this sad Grief, most noble *Timon,*
The Senators of *Athens* greet thee with
Their Love, and do with one consenting Voice
Intreat thee back to *Athens.*
Tim I thank 'em, and would send them back the Plague,
Could I but catch it for 'em.
Ælius. The Gods forbid! they love thee most sincerely.
Tim. I will return 'em the same Love they bear me.
Nic Forget, most noble *Timon:* they are sorry
They should deny thee thy Request; they do
Confess their Fault; the publick Body,
Which seldom does recant, confesses it.
Cleon. And has sent us——
Tim A very scurvy Sample of that Body!
Phæax. Oh my good Lord! we've ever lov'd you best
Of all Mankind.
Thras. And equal with our selves.
Isid. Our Hearts and Souls were ever fixt upon thee.
Isand. We would stake our Lives for you.
Phæax We are all griev'd to think you shou'd
So misinterpret our best Loves.
Cleon Which shall continue ever firm to you.
Tim Good Men! you much surprize me, even to Tears;
Lend me a Fool's Heart, and Womens Eyes,
And I'll beweep these Comforts, worthy Lords.
Nic. We beg your Honour will interpret fairly.
Phæax. The Senate has reserv'd some special Dignities
Now vacant, to confer on you   They pray
You will return, and be their Captain,
Allow'd with absolute Command.   *Nic.*

Nic. Wild *Alcibiades* approaches *Athens*
With all his Force, and like a savage Bear,
Roots up his Country's Peace; we humbly beg
Thy just Assistance.

Phæax. We all know thou'rt worthy,
And hast oblig'd thy Country heretofore
Beyond Return.

Ælius. Therefore, good noble Lord——

Tim. I tell you, Lords,
If *Alcibiades* kill my Countrymen,
Let *Alcibiades* know this of *Timon*,
That *Timon* cares not: But if he sack fair *Athens*,
And take our goodly aged Men by th' Beards,
Giving up purest Virgins to the Stain
Of beastly mad-brain'd War; then let him know,
In Pity of the Aged and the Young,
I cannot chuse but tell him that I care not,
And let him take't at worse; for their Swords care not,
While you have Throats to answer: For my self,
There's not a Knive in all th' unruly Camp,
But I do love, and value more than the
Most rev'rend Throat in *Athens*, tell 'em so!
Be *Alcibiades* your Plague, ungrateful Villains!

Phæax. Oh my good Lord! you think too hardly of us.

Ælius. Hang him! there's no Hopes of him.

Nic. He'll ne'er return; he truly is *Misanthropos*.

Phæax. You have Gold, my Lord, will you not serve
Your Country with some of it?

Tim. O my dear Country! I do recant
Commend me kindly to the Senate, tell 'em,
If they will come all in one Body to me,
And follow my Advice, they shall be welcome.

Nic. I am sure they will, my noble Lord.

Tim. I will instruct 'em how to ease their Griefs,
Their Fears of hostile Strokes, their Aches, Losses,
Their covetous Pangs, with other incident Throes
That Nature's fragil Vessels must sustain
In Life's uncertain Voyage.

Phæax. How my good Lord! this kind Care is noble.

Tim. Why even thus——

I will

I will point out the most convenient Trees
In all this Wood, to hang themselves upon.
And so farewel, ye covetous fawning Slaves begone!
Let me not see the Face of Man more, I
Had rather see a Tyger fasting———

   Nic He's lost to all our Purposes.

   Phæax. Let's send a Party out of *Athens* to him,
To force him to confess his Treasure;
And put him to the Torture, if he will not.

   Aic. It will do well! let's away.   [*Drums.*

   Ælius. What Drums are those?

   Phæax. They must belong to *Alcibiades.*
To Horse, and fly, or we shall chance be taken.   [*Ex.*

   Tim. Go fly, *Evandra*, to my Cave, or thou
May'st suffer by the Rage of lustful Villains.

   Enter Alcibiades *with* Phryne *and* Thais, *two Whores.*

   Alcib. Command a Halt, and send a Messenger
To summon *Athens* from me!
What art thou there? speak.   [thee,

   Tim A two-legg'd Beast, as thou art, Cankers gnaw
For shewing me the Face of Man again

   Alcib. Is Man so hateful to thee! what art thou?

   Tim I am *Misanthropos!* I hate Mankind:
And for thy Part, I wish thou wer't a Dog,
That I might love thee something.
But now I think on't, thou art going
Against yon cursed Town: Go on! It is
A worthy Cause

   Alcib Oh *Timon!* now I know thee, I am sorry
For thy Misfortunes; and hope a little time
Will give me Occasion to redress 'em.

   Tim I will not alter my Condition
For all you e'er shall conquer; no, go on,
Paint with Man's Blood the Earth: Dye it well.
Religious Canons, Civil Laws are cruel,
What then must War be?

   Alcib. How came the noble *Timon* by this Change?

   Tim As the Moon does by wanting Light to give,
And then renew I could not like the Moon,
There were no Suns to borrow of.

                          Alcib

Alcib. What Friendship shall I do thee?

Tim. Why, promise me Friendship, and perform none.
If thou wilt not promise, thou art no Man.
If thou dost perform, thou art none neither.

Alcib. I am griev'd to see thy Misery.

Tim. Thou saw'st it when I was rich.

Alcib. Then was a happy Time.

Tim. As thine is now, abus'd by a Brace of Harlots.
What, do'st thou fight with Women by thy Side?

Alcib. No; but after all the Toils and Hazards of the
Day with Men, I refresh my self at Night with Women.

Tim. These false Whores of thine have more Destruction
in 'em than thy Sword

Phry. Thou art a Villain to say so——

Thais. Is this he, that was the *Athenian* Minion?
A snarling Rascal.

Tim. Be Whores still; they love you not that use you,
Employ all your Salt Hours to ruine Youth,
Soften their Manners into a Lethargy
Of Sense and Action

Phry. Hang thee, Monster! We are not Whores, we
are Mistresses to *Alcibiades*

Tim. The right Name is Whore, do not miscal it;
Ye have been so to many

Thais. Out on you, Dog.

Alcib. Pray pardon him,
His Wits are lost in his Calamities.
I have but little Gold, but here's some for thee.

Tim. Keep it, I cannot eat it.

Alcib. Wilt thou go 'gainst *Athens* with me?

Tim. If ye were Beasts, I'd go with ye;
But I'll not herd with Men, yet I love thee
Better than all Men, because thou wer't born
To ruin thy base Country.

Alcib. I've sent to summon *Athens*, if she obeys not
I'll lay her on a Heap.

Tim. It were a glorious Act! go on, go on;
Here's Gold for thee, stay, I'll fetch thee more.

Alcib. What Mystery is this! where should he have this?

Tim. Here's more Gold and Jewels! go on,

D d   Be

Be a devouring Plague, let not
Thy Sword skip one, spare thou no Sex or Age:
Pity not honour'd Age for his white Beard,
He's an Usurer, strike the counterfeit Matron,
It is her Habit only that is honest,
Her self's a Bawd; let not the Virgin's Cheek
Make soft thy Sword, nor Milk-Paps giving Suck;
Spare not the Babe, whose dimpled Smiles
From Fools exhaust their Mercy; think 'twill be
A Rogue, or Whore, ere long, if thou should'st spare it.
Put Armour on thy Eyes and Ears, whose Proof,
Nor Yells of Mothers, Maids, nor crying Babes,
Nor Sight of Priests in holy Vestments bleeding,
Shall pierce one jot.

    Phry Hast thou more Gold good *Timon?* give us some,
    Thais What Pity 'tis he should be thus melancholy!
He is a fine Person now
    Tim Oh flattering Whores! but that I'm sure you will
Do Store of Mischief, I'd not give you any:
Here! be sure you be Whores still,
And who with pious Breath seeks to convert ye,
Be strong in Whore, allure and burn him up,
Thatch your thin Skulls with Burthens from the Dead,
Some that were hang'd no matter,
Wear them! betray with them, Whore still;
Paint till a Horse may mire upon your Faces———
A Pox on Wrinkles, I say
    Thais Well, more Gold, say what thou wilt.
    Tim Sow your Consumptions in the Bones of Men;
Dry up their Marrows, pain their Shins
And Shoulders Crack the Lawyer's Voice, that he
May never bawl, and plead false Title more
Entice the lustful and dissembling Priests,
That scold against the Quality of Flesh,
And not believe themselves; I am not well
Here's more, ye proud, lascivious, rampant Whores.
Do you damn others, and let this damn you,
And Ditches be all your Death-beds and your Graves.
    Por More Counsel, and more Money, bounteous *Timon.*
    Tim. More Whore! more Mischief first,

                I've

I've given you Earneſt.

Alcib. We but diſturb him ! farewel,
If I thrive wel', I'll viſit thee again

Tim If I thrive well, I ne'er ſhall ſee thee more :
I feel Death's happy Stroke upon me now,
He has laid his icy Hands upon me at length ,
He will not let me go again, Farewel
Confound *Athens*, and then thy ſelf   [*Exit* Tim.

Alcib Now march, ſound Trumpets, and beat Drums,
And let the Terror of the Noiſe invade
Th' ungrateful, cowardly, uſurious Senate.   [*Exeunt.*

Enter Nicias, Ælius, Cleon, Thraſillus, Iſidore, Iſander,
upon the Works of Athens

Nic. What ſhall we do to appeaſe his Rage ?
He has an Army able to devour us.

Phæax We muſt e'en humbly bow our Necks, that he
May tread on 'em

Ælius He is a Man of eaſy Nature, ſoon won by
Soothings

Nic I tremble left he ſhould revenge our Sentence.

Iſid. If we ſhou'd reſiſt, he'll level *Athens.*

Iſand And then Woe to our ſelves,
Our Wives and Daughters.

Nic. What will become of you and me *Phæax ?*
We have been Enemies to him long.   I tremble for it.

Phæax Let us appear moſt forward in delivering up
the Town to him.

Nic. If we reſiſt, he'll uſe a Conqu'ror's Power,
And nothing then will 'ſcape the Fury of
The headſtrong Soldiers ; we muſt all ſubmit.
See, he approaches.   Theſe Drums and Trumpets
Strike Terror in me ! Heav'n help all.

Enter Herald, *then* Alcibiades *and his Army,*

Alcib. What Anſwer make they to my Summons ?

Herald They are on the Works to treat with you.

Alcib There's a white Flag ! let us approach 'em.
Hoa ! you on the Works ! give me and my Army Entrance,
Or I'll let looſe the Fury of my Soldiers,
And make you all a Prey to Spoil and Rapine ,
And ſuch a Flame I'll light about your Ears

Shall make *Greece* tremble.

   Nic My noble Lord, we mean nothing leſs

   Pbeax Only we beg your Honour will forgive us.

   Nic We've been ungrateful, and are much aſham'd on't;
Your Lordſhip ſhall tread upon our Necks, if you think
We cannot but condemn our ſelves,   [good;
But we appeal to your known Mercy and
Your Generoſity

   Phæax March, noble Lord, into our City,
With all the Banners ſpread, we are thy Slaves.

   Ælus Your Footſtools

   Iſid Whatever you will make us.

   Tbraſ Enter our City, noble *Alcibiades,* but leave
Your Rage behind you

   Iſand Set but your Foot againſt our Gates, and they
Shall open——ſo you will enter like a Friend.

   Alcib Open the Gates, without Capitulations,
For if I ſet my Battering Rams to work,
You muſt expect no Mercy

   Nic We will, my good Lord——

   [*They all come down.* Nicias *preſents* Alcibiades *the*
     Keys upon his Knees.

Our Lives and Fortunes now are in thy Hands;
But we fly to thy Mercy for Protection.

   Alcib. You merit as much Mercy as you ſhew'd
To *Thraſibulus*; ſuch monſtrous Ingratitude
Will make your villainous Names grow odious
To all the Race of Men, but to your ſelves
To whom Vertue is ſo

   Phæax. 'Twas the whole Senate's Voice.

   Alcib A Senate! a Den of Thieves! I little thought
When I wreſted the Pow'r from the Rabble,
To give it you, you would be worſe than they;
But moſt of you deſerve the Oſtraciſm:
Some of you are ſuch Rogues, you'd ſhame the Gibbet.

   Nic Good my Lord, tread on our Necks but pardon us.

   Phæax We'll be your Slaves, if you'll forgive us.

   Alcib Can you forgive *Thraſibulus* when he's dead?
Muſt we be us'd thus after our frequent Hazards, and
Our Toils, hard weary Marching, Watching, Faſting,

                     Such

Such dreadful Hardſhips; lying out ſuch Nights
A Beaſt could not abide without a Covert,
And all for purſy, lazy Knaves, that ſnort
In Peace at home, and wallow in their Bags ?
Muſt we, the Bulwarks of our Country, be
Thus us'd !

 Phæax Ceaſe to reproach us, my good Lord.

 Ælius We are full of Shame and Guilt.

 Cleon Pardon us, good *Alcibiades*

 Thraſ We heartily repent.

 Iſid We'll kiſs thy Feet, good Lord

 Iſand Do with us what thou wilt

 Alcib You ſix of the foremoſt here muſt meet me
In the ANUX, where I'll order the PRITANES
To aſſemble all the People———
And on your Knees preſent your ſelves
With Halters 'bout your Necks.

 Phæax Oh my good Lord !

 Alcib Diſpute it not; for by the Gods, if you
Fail in this Point, I'll hang ye all,
Rifle your Houſes, and extirpate all
Your Race———March on
Give Order that not a Man ſhall break his Ranks,
Or ſhall offend the regular Courſe of Juſt.ce,
On Penalty of Death—March on.   [*Ex Omnes.*

  Enter Timon *and* Evandra, *coming out of the Cave.*

 Evan Oh my dear Lord! why do you ſtoop and bend,
Like Flowers o'er-charg'd with Dew, whoſe yielding Stalks
Cannot ſupport 'em? I have a Cordial, which
Will much revive thy Spirits.

 Tim No, ſweet *Evandra*,
I have taken the beſt Cordial, Death, which now
Kindly begins to work about my Vitals;
I feel him, he comforts me at Heart

 Evan. Oh, my dear *Timon* ! muſt we then part ?
That I ſhould live to ſee this fatal Day !
Had Death but ſeiz'd me firſt, I h d been happy.

 Tim My poor *Evandra*, lead me to my Grave,
Leſt Death o'ertake me---he purſues me hard .
He's cloſe upon me 'Tis the laſt Office thou

       Can'ſt

Can'ft do for *Timon.*

   Evan Hard, ftubborn Heart,
Wilt thou not break yet ? Death, why art thou coy
To me that court thee ?

   Tim Lay me gently down
In my laft Tenement.   Death's the trueft Friend,
That will not flatter, but deals plainly with us.
So, now my weary Pilgrimage on Earth
Is almoft finifh'd : Now, my beft *Evandra,*
I charge thee, by our Loves, our mutual Loves,
Live ! and live happy after me , and if
A Thought of *Timon* comes into thy Mind,
And brings a Tear from thee, let fome Diverfion
Banifh it quickly——ftrive to forget me

   Evan Oh *Timon !* Think'ft thou, I am fuch a Coward
I will not keep my Word? Death fhall not part us.

   Tim If thou'lt not promife me to live, I cannot
Refign my Life in Peace, I will be with thee
After my Death , my Soul fhall follow thee
And hover ftill about thee, and guard thee from
All Harm

   Evan Life is the greateft Harm when thou art dead.

   Tim Can'ft thou forgive thy *Timon,* who involv'd
Thee in his fad Calamities ?

   Evan It is a Blefling to fhare any thing
With thee   O thou look'ft pale, thy Countenance changes,
O whither art thou going

   Tim To my laft Home   I charge thee, live, *Evandra ,*
Thou lov'ft me not, if thou wilt not obey me ;
Thou only, deareft, kind, conftant Thing on Earth !
Farewel.   [*Dies.*

   Evan He's gone ! he's gone ! would all the World were
I muft make Hafte, or I fhall not o'ertake   [fo !
Him in his Flight   *Timon,* I come, ftay for me,
Farewel bafe World   [*Stabs herself   Dies.*
Enter Alcibiades, Phrinias, *and* Thais, *his Officers and
   Soldiers, and his Train, the Senators.   The People by de-
   grees affembling.*   •

Enter Meliffa.

Mel. My *Alcibiades !* welcome ! doubly welcome !

                                                          The

The Joys of Love and Conqueſt ever bleſs thee,
Wonder and Terror of Mankind, and Joy
Of Woman-kind: Now thy *Meliſſa*'s happy,
She has liv'd to ſee the utmoſt Day ſhe wiſh'd for,
Her *Alcibiades* return with Conqueſt
O'er this ungrateful City; and but that
I every Day heard thou wert marching hither,
I had been with thee long ere this.

    Alcib What gay, vain prating Thing is this?
    Mel. How my Lord! do you queſtion who *Meliſſa* is?
And give her ſuch foul Titles?
    Alcib. I know *Meliſſa*, and therefore give her ſuch
Titles; for when the Senate baniſh'd me,
She would not ſee me, tho' upon her Knees
Before ſhe had ſworn eternal Love to me;
I ſee thy Snares too plain to be caught now.
    Mel. I ne'er refus'd to ſee you, Heav'n can witneſs!
Whoever told you ſo betray'd me baſely.
Not ſee you! ſure there's not a Sight on Earth
I'd chuſe before you· You make me aſtoniſh'd!
    Alcib. All this you ſwore to *Timon*; and next Day
Deſpis'd him——I have been inform'd
Of all your Falſhood, and I hate thee for't;
I have Whores, good honeſt faithful Whores!
Good Antidotes againſt thy Poiſon—Love;
Thy baſe falſe Love; and tell me, is not one
Kind, faithful, loving Whore, better than
A Thouſand, baſe, ill-natur'd honeſt Women?
    Mel I never thought I ſhould have liv'd to hear
This from my *Alcibiades*.
    Alcib Do not weep,
Since I once lik'd thee, I'll do ſomething for thee:
I have a Corporal that has ſerv'd me well,
I will prefer you to him.
    Mel How have I merited this Scorn—farewel,
I'll never ſee you more.   [*Ex.*
    Alcib. I hope you will not.
        [*Enter Soldiers with drawn Swords, hauling*
            in Apem ntus.
How now! what means this Violence?

                         1 *Sold.*

1 Sold. My Lord! this fnarling villainous Philofopher,
with open Mouth rail'd at the Army, he faid the General was a Villain. Shall we cut his Throat?

Alcib. No, touch him not! unhand him!
Why, *Apementus*, did'ft thou call me Villain?

Apem. I always fpeak my Thoughts Not all
The Swords o'th' Army bent againft my Throat
Can fright me from the Truth——

Alcib. Why do'ft thou think I am one?

Apem. 'Tis true, that this bafe Town deferves thy
And all the Terror and the Punifhment   [Scourge,
Thou can'ft inflict upon it · The Deed is good,
But yet thou do'ft it ill; private Revenge,
Bafe Paffion, headftrong Luft, incite thee to it,
Had they not banifh'd thee, thou would'ft have fuffer'd
Wrong ftill to profper, and th' infulting Tyrants
To thrive, fwell, and grow fat with their Oppreffion,
And wouldft have join'd in them

Alcib. Thou rail'ft too much for a Philofopher

Apem. Nay, frown not, Lord, I fear thee not, nor
    love thee;
All thy good Parts thou drown'ft in Vice and Riot,
In Paffion and Vain-glory How proud art thou
Of all thy Conquefts——when a poor Rabble
Of idle Rogues, who elfe had been in Jails,
Perform'd 'em for thee, how falfe is Soldier's Honour!
With Drums and Trumpets, and in the Face of Day
With daring Impudence Men go to murther Mankind.
But in the greateft Actions of their Lives,
The getting Men, they fneak and hide themfelves
I'th' dark, I fcorn your Folly and your Madnefs,

Alcib. Thou art a fnarling Cur

1 Sold. Shall I run him through?

Alcib. Hold

Apem. I fear thee not

Alcib. My ever honour'd *Socrates* favour'd thee,
And for his Sake I fpare thee

Apem. How much did *Socrates* lofe his Pains in thee?
Had'ft thou obferv'd his Principles, thoud'ft been honeft.

Enter

Enter Nicias, Thrasillus, Phæax, Isidore, Isander, Ælius, *and* Cleon, *with Halters about their Necks.*

Nicias We come, my noble Lord, at thy Command,
And thus we humbly kneel before thy Mercy.

Phæax Spare our Lives, and we'll employ 'em in
Thy Service, worthy *Alcibiades.*

Alcib Do you acknowledge you're ungrateful Knaves?

All. We do.

Alcib And that you have used me basely

All We have, but we are very sorry.

Alcib. I should do well to hang you for the Death
Of my brave Officer, but Thousand such base Lives
As yours would not weigh with his! Go, ye have
Your Liberty. And now the People are assembled,
I will declare my Intentions towards them.

[*He ascends the Pulpit.*

My Fellow-Citizens! I will not now upbraid
You for the unjust Sentence past upon me,
In the Return of which I have subdu'd
Your Enemies, and all revolted Places,
Made you victorious both at Land and Sea,
And with continual Toil and numberless Dangers
Stretcht out the Bounds of your Dominions far
Above your Hopes or Expectations.
I'll not recount the many Enterprizes
No *Grecian* can be ignorant of 'Tis enough
You know how I have serv'd you Now it remains
I farther should declare myself; I come
First to free you good Citizens of *Athens*
From the most insupportable Yokes
Of your Four Hundred Tyrants; and then next
To claim my own Estate, which has unjustly
By them been kept from me that rais'd them.
I do confess, I in revenge of your Decree
Against me, set up them, but never thought
They would have been such cursed Tyrants to you,
Till now, they have gone on, and fill'd the Time
With most licentious Acts, making their Wills,
Their base corrupted Wills, the Scope of Justice,
While you in vain groan'd under all your Sufferings.
Thus

Thus when a few fhall lord it o'er the reft,
They govern for themfelves, and not the People.
They rob and pill from them, from thence t'increafe
Their private Stores ; but when the Government
Is in the Body of the People, they
Will do themfelves no Harm ; therefore henceforth
I do pronounce the Government fhall devolve
Upon the People, and may Heav'n profper 'em.

> [*People fhout, and cry,* Alcibiades ! Alcibiades !
> *Long live* Alcibiades ! *Liberty, Liberty,* &c.
> [Alcib. *defcends.*

Enter Meffenger.

Meff. My noble Lord ! I went as you commanded,
And found Lord *Timon* dead, and his *Evandra*
Stabb'd, and juft by him lying in his Tomb,
On which was this infcription.

Alcib. I'll read it.

> *Here lies a wretched Coarfe, of wretched Soul bereft,*
> *Timon my Name, a Plague confume you Caitiffs left.*

Poor *Timon !* I once knew thee the moft flourifhing Man
Of all th' *Athenians,* and thou ftill hadft been fo,
Had not thefe fmiling, flattering Knaves devour'd thee,
And murder'd thee with bafe Ingratitude.
His Death pull'd on the poor *Evandra*'s too ;
That Miracle of Conftancy in Love.
Now all repair to their refpective Homes,
Their feveral Trades, their Bus'nefs and Diverfions ;
And whilft I guard you from your active Foes,
And fight your Battles, be you fecure at home.

> *May* Athens *flourifh with a lafting Peace,*
> *And may its Wealth and Power e'er increafe.*

> [*All the People fhout and cry,* Alcibiades ! Alcibiades !
> *Liberty ! Liberty !* &c

E P I

EPILOGUE.

IF there were Hopes that ancient, solid Wit
Might please within our new fantastick Pit,
This Play might then support the Critick's Shock,
This Scien grafted upon Shakespear's *Stock ,*
For, join'd with his, our Poet's Parts might thrive,
Kept by the Vertue of his Sap alive.
Tho' now no more substantial English *Plays*
Than good old Hospitality you praise ;
The Time shall come, when true old Sense shall rise
In Judgment over all your Vanities
Sight Kickshaw Wit o'th' Stage, French *Meat at Feasts,*
Now daily tantalize the hungry Guests ;
While the old English *Chine us'd to remain,*
And many hungry Onsets would sustain
At these thin Feasts each Morsel's swallow'd down,
And ev'ry Thing but the Guests Stomach's gone.
At these new fashion'd Feasts you've but a Taste,
With Meat or Wit you scarce can break a Fast.
This Jantee *Slightness to the* French *we owe,*
And that makes all slight Wits admire 'em so.
They're of one Level, and with little Pains
The frothy Poet good Reception gains ;
But to hear English *Wit there's Use of Brains.*
Tho' Sparks *to imitate the* French *think fit,*
In Want of Learning, Affectation, Wit,
And, which is most, in Clothes ; we'll ne'er submit.
Their Ships or Plays o'er ours shall ne'er advance,
For our third Rates shall match the first of France.
With English *Judges this may bear the Test,*
Who will for Shakespear's *Part forgive the rest.*
The Sparks judge but as they hear others say ;
They cannot think enough to mind a Play.

They

EPILOGUE.

They to catch Ladies (which they dr y's at) come;
Or 'cause they cannot read or think at home;
Each here doux yeux and am'rous Looks imparts,
Levels Crevats and Perriwigs at Hearts;
Yet they themselves more than the Ladies mind,
And but for Vanity wou'd have 'em kind.

No Passion,
But for their own dear Persons, them can move;
Th' admire themselves too much to be in Love
Nor Wit nor Beauty their hard Hearts can strike,
Who only their own Sense or Persons like
But to the Men of Wit our Poet flies,
To save him from Wit's mortal Enemies:
Since for his Friends he has the best of those,
Guarded by them, he fears not little Foes
And with each Mistress we must Favour find,
They for Evandra's Sake will sure be kind,
At least all those to constant Love inclin'd.

F I N I S.

Printed in the USA
CPSIA information can be obtained
at www.ICGtesting.com
LVHW012221251123
764515LV00033B/306